PREFACE *to the* PAST

By James Branch Cabell

BIOGRAPHY OF THE LIFE OF MANUEL
PREFACE TO THE PAST

By Branch Cabell

SMIRT
SMITH

THESE RESTLESS HEADS
SPECIAL DELIVERY
LADIES AND GENTLEMEN

PREFACE *to the* PAST

by

JAMES BRANCH CABELL

"He dwells, with a gently lingering, long-drawn music of tone, upon old, faded things: philosophies once triumphant, fashions once thought final, airs and graces long passed away, and music never heard now."

WILDSIDE PRESS: MMIII

PREFACE TO THE PAST

Published by
Wildside Press
P.O. Box 301
Holicong, PA 18928-0301 U.S.A.
www.wildsidepress.com

To

MANUEL'S BEST FRIEND

Gaily we shared long labors, each with each,
Until at last there was not any showing
Your thought from mine, your speaking from my
speech.

Hardly we knew, that had no need of knowing,
One from another; and all went to lend
Life to our Manuel—and to his going
Thus far, with you alone, past Storisende.

CONTENTS

"MERE HOMESPUN MEMORIES"

*"Whosoever goes in quest of instruction,
let him fish for it where it is to be found;
there is nothing I so little profess. These
are mere homespun memories, by which
I do not pretend to discover things, but to
lay open my book."*

"Mere Homespun Memories"

B E IT prologized that when the Storisende edition of the Biography of the Life of Manuel was prepared in 1927-30, then not merely was the complete text of the Biography rewritten, with the candors permissible in a limited edition, and considerable new matter added to most of the volumes, but also to each of the revised volumes was affixed its own special, informal, and rather garrulous commentary in the form of an Author's Note. In this present book, thrift has collected these twenty commentaries, now "out of print," as being equally applicable to the unrevised text of the yet current Kalki edition.

Here and there may be found a reference which applies only to the definitive text; but such references are not many enough to mislead a tolerably attentive reader. For the rest, the chief purpose of these commentaries is two-fold: to explain, first, the place of the discussed volume in the structure of the entire Biography; and to explain, secondly, the circumstances in which this volume came to be written, as well as the circumstances in which it was published: to explain, that is, the special functions and the special origins of each volume. These are "points" which in their connection with the Kalki edition, it is believed, may appear equally pointed.

Throughout these commentaries some verbal changes have been necessitated in order that these individually prefatory papers might be put together so as to make a volume annotating the Biography as a whole; it has been thought well to add a commentary, which is virtually new, upon *The Witch-Woman* trilogy; and it has seemed preferable to list out of canonical order the commentary upon *The Lineage of Lichfield,* so that the protagonist of the Biography might be made apparent, rather more insistently, at outset.

To the commentaries are added five notes which will be found self-explanatory. Three of these notes, concerning the Biography in general, have seen earlier service in the disguise of prefaces to three volumes of the Biography in a special illustrated version. The *Addenda as to Jurgen* is printed for the first time. The note upon *Townsend of Lichfield,* the one item which in part has appeared elsewhere than in small "limited" editions, has been included so that the reader might have here in complete form all commentaries upon the Biography as a complete whole which have seemed needful to the Biography's maker.

INDEED, to include in this book the note upon *Town-send of Lichfield* is a tribute demanded by the main requirement of every author. I mean, of course, self-conceit. In this note (most of which was first published in the *American Mercury*, for June 1929, and later, in the autumn of 1929, reissued as a "colophon" to *The Way of Ecben*) it was my melancholy privilege to play the but too successful prophet, by pointing out that the American writers most looked up to during the 'twenties were now due, if not exactly to decrease in all famousness, at best to add nothing further to their repute; and that, in brief, their pre-eminence was over.

To-day that seems fairly obvious. Now that my unwilling prophecy has been verified, and its truth turned into a gray truism by so many journalists all harping, with a relish superior to mine, upon the collapse of this entire literary generation, like a punctured balloon, it seems that the oncoming of this collapse ought to have been foreseeable by everybody. . . . And to that I agree. To anticipate its oncoming, and indeed the approximate year of its oncoming, was needed only a sane weighing of history's sad mania for self-repetition.

Yet in 1929, I can assure you, an announcement of this collapse was regarded as flat nonsense, and as cloudily unpatriotic nonsense, in I know not how many derisory newspaper articles which purported to review *The Way of Ecben*. No one of these articles said anything about *The Way of Ecben.* Instead, with a proud indignation which at the same instant spurned biology and put history out of doors, they expounded upon the "untrue" and the "defeatist" doctrine of the book's "colophon." I was refuted, for that matter, with a large deal of firsthand evidence, inasmuch as some of the authors who were immediately concerned made noble jaunts into print, to deny my nonsense and to concede candidly the full retention of their literary powers for an indefinite period to come.

Well, but it is not that I would boast. The pudding has since then been subjected to its proverbial proof. I think—with nobody whatever contradicting me nowadays, so far as I know—that the last seven years have but too well borne out my unwilling prediction. I do not believe that any American writer of the elder generation, or, let us say, any tolerably gifted American writer now fairly upwards of fifty, has mounted in critical esteem since 1929. I am quite certain that no one of them has surpassed the best work which he or she produced prior to 1929.

Yet—and this, look you, is my true point—that no other outcome was ever at all probable, I am equally certain. It is a conviction born of hale reasons which you may find stated in the latter part of this note on *Townsend of Lichfield*—a paper wherein, a long seven years ago, I made plain those causes which had led me at fifty to complete the Biography, and so far to change my name as an author as to distinguish plainly between the Biography and all writings thereafter published by me unrelated to the Biography.

I PAUSE here. And I think I had better not continue. So I shall not speak any further as to the present, somewhat tragic plight of my own out-of-date generation in American letters, now that time taxes our glories in the same large piratical spirit with which the Federal Government touches our material earnings.

Otherwise, in my next paragraph would gross human nature urge me to wallow in the ignoble, and the infuriating-to-all-its-hearers and the extremely delicious, human pleasure of remarking, "I told you so." I dare not not avoid that temptation. I will not wallow. With a self-restraint rather rare among justified prophets, I prefer to drop this theme in this paragraph.

INSTEAD, I pursue a theme more personal. It was through this note upon *Townsend of Lichfield* that in 1929 I announced my intention to publish no more books, so I am told. And not seldom do I hear about this. Indeed, it is a bit of public knowledge which some while since assumed perpetuity: if it nowadays

be not quite amaranthine, it at any rate ranks as a
hardy perennial, or (to be wholly accurate) it as yet
flourishes, in the tropical imagination of many book
reviewers, like an orchid, without the least need of
any sensible root.

I confess to some twinges of wonderment whensoever I encounter this gaudily imbecile misstatement. Yet just so often as I happen through force
of habit to bring out a new book, then I do encounter this misstatement, over and still over again,
in the provincial press. That fact is discouraging, it
is even sombre, when you consider its bearings upon
the mentality of our press—which, as is well known,
remains also the most glorious palladium of our
democratic liberties. So if I speak lightly about this
fact, I nevertheless speak (as befits a true patriot)
between gnashed teeth, in uncontrolled rage, with
my lips suitably foaming. I feel deeply, I can assure
you, that a palladium, whatever it may happen to
be, ought not to be idiotic.

I feel even some personal animus in the matter.
I weary of being termed a liar. For, so far as this
note at all concerned my future plans, it did but remark, in language such as I still think to be comprehensible by a person of moderate intelligence
(from which class I would not utterly exclude the
intelligentsia of provincial journalism), that the
Biography of the Life of Manuel was now finished;

and that in consequence no more would be added by me to the Biography of the Life of Manuel.

But do you yourself, entering affably into the cliché, come as a Daniel to judgment . . . "I determined, therefore, now some ten years ago," I declared, in 1929, "to finish the Biography before I had passed fifty, if it were granted me to live that long; and thereafter to add no line to, and to change in nothing, the Biography. The Biography of the Life of Manuel seems now, to my partial gaze, a completed performance." . . . I here quote verbatim from the exact text of my "colophon," as it appeared, in 1929, in *The Way of Ecben*; and if any less equivocal statements have ever been made, in quite simple English, I do not know of them. They still seem to me to express the meaning I intended—which was that I would add no more to the long book about Manuel's life, because the book was now finished in accord with my original design, in accord with its architect's blue-prints.

However, now I think of it, anyone who is so far interested in this matter as to continue writing about it thus time-wastingly, for seven whole years, can discover for himself "just what I did say" in this note. He, the intrepid innovator, might, it is barely possible, do this by reading my statements before he commented on them any further. And so to all habitual scoffers at my inconstancy I make bold to suggest this relatively unimaginative method of approaching my note about *Townsend of Lichfield*.

YET it is not upon this note I would close here. Of my contemporaries and my critics in once current letters I have spoken thus far without as yet expressing my main feeling toward them all nowadays. That feeling is, very really and very deeply, a feeling of gratitude. Now that I preface a past which they in particular have helped to make interesting, I regard my aforetime playfellows, upon both sides, with frank thankfulness. We have diverted one another hugeously. And I would not demand of them, any more than would they (I am sure) of me, omniscience. I consider that for omniscience to take part in any game, among human fallible opponents, would be plain cheating.

So it seems to me nowadays quite enough that no great while ago we writing persons, upon both sides, fought out, in our books, our magazines and our newspapers, a fine, rough-and-tumble game which we high-heartedly called "a literary movement." That "movement" was unexampled in American annals. It was noted even by the unprofessedly literary; it was talked about by responsible citizens; it was remarked on in foreign lands with a condescension virtually civil. Not merely did we produce competent writers in that loud-lunged era: we actually read them. In brief, bookishness boomed, during "the revolt of the 'twenties."

The strength of that many-sided "movement," fatally weakened by the deaths of Frances Newman and of Elinor Wylie late in 1928, came to an end (so I believe) in 1929, with much other wreckage. If our "movement" had so far shared in the chief trait of most human doings as not to be permanently important, it had at any rate been pleasurably exciting; and its yet living participants might well part in all friendship, the game being over.

Such at least was my own frame of mind (one that still stays unchanged) when in 1929 I concluded the Biography with an expounding of its design, with a setting forth of its architecture, in the papers which follow. Such was my thinking when I put together these commentaries. Then I made a discovery.

MY DISCOVERY was that, in writing so much about the Biography, I seemed to have written a very great deal more, not exactly about "the revolt of the 'twenties," but rather about the entire genteel, gaunt, starved, fever-stricken, rebellious literary era, between 1902 and 1930, during which both "the revolt of the 'twenties" and the Biography took shape and reached their shared ending. In setting down faithfully all the vagaries of that era's taboos, and of its transient criteria, and of its fleeting dictators, as one by one these vagaries had touched (or had been evaded by) me and my "romantic" books, I had made a fairly long book which everywhere was sound "realism." In part it did preface the Biography: but in its every sentence it prefaced a past era—quaint, dead, incredible, yet once actual,—and about that era in American letters it told you the truth, literally, if at times with a casualness, speaking as an eye-witness.

I, in brief, and in dissent from my own convictions, had been betrayed, after all, into writing "realism." Unintentionally, I had constructed a well-documented history and a staid chronicle untarnished by any least breath of the imaginative. Such was my odd discovery when in putting together these commentaries I came to take leave of the Biography, and of my twenty-eight years' playing with it.

The COMMENTARIES

"*The fancy of a perpetual life, sweeping together ten thousand experiences, is an old one; and modern thought has conceived the idea of humanity as wrought upon by, and summing up in itself, all modes of thought and life. Here is an embodiment of the old fancy, a symbol of the modern idea.*"

Beyond Life

TO THE very best, if irrelevant, judgment of
the book's author, *Beyond Life* ought to be regarded as a Prologue to the Biography of the Life
of Manuel. And *Beyond Life*, therefore, attempts
to introduce, and to describe, through their informal
discussion, all the main themes of the Biography,—
of that rather long Biography, divided into twenty
sections, concerned with the life of Dom Manuel of
Poictesme, not only as that life was lived by him, but
also as that life was perpetuated in his children, and
through the descendants of these children, down to
our present time.

In particular does *Beyond Life* attempt to outline
the three general attitudes toward human existence
which have been adopted or illustrated, and in some
instances blended, by the many descendants of
Manuel. I mean, the chivalrous attitude, the gallant
attitude, and what I can only describe as the poetic
attitude. The descendants of Manuel have at various
times very variously viewed life as a testing; as a
toy; and as raw material. Some of them have sought

during their existence upon earth to become admirable, even by the one true test of your private thoughts while lying awake at night; others have endeavored simply, or it might be somewhat complexly, to enjoy life while life lasted; and yet others have tried, through the medium of art, to create something more durable than life. The outcome the Biography records. For the rest, it appeared to me when I came to rewrite *Beyond Life* for the Storisende edition of my books, some ten years after the first writing of this special volume, *Beyond Life* does raise, more or less definitely, nearly all the dissimilar problems moiled over and, heaven knows, left quite unsettled, by Manuel and by the descendants of Manuel.

Yet it is John Charteris, I would have you note, who speaks my Prologue, and not I. *Beyond Life* is a book of his notions, about a great many age-old questions which have perplexed human beings ever since human beings began to perplex angels, rather than a book of my notions. And I, for one, incline to regard the notions of John Charteris with not a whit more of long-faced gravity than he accorded them. He, as a thorough-going Economist, takes seriously this sole notion, that all human ideas are probably incorrect about everything. It is certain we have no way of checking off the correctness of any human ideas. All human ideas—it follows in the hidebound creed of the Economist—should be valued only as the playthings with which one purchases diversion. One plays with them during the night season of a not-yet-ended Walburga's Eve, which is called "living,"—and during which almost anything is rather more than likely to happen.

The utmost which Charteris asserts for his many notions is, thus, that, in the lighted snug place which temporarily is his home, having the sun and the moon also for its candles, they enable him to dispose of an uncertain but an assuredly not large number of hours rather pleasurably; and to forget, for a while at least, the ambiguities and the darkness, along with the vaguely felt malevolence too, of that not-yet-ended Walburga's Eve which encompasses his frail pleasant home everywhere, within dreadfully quick reaching distance. That—still I cite for you the creed of the Economist—that is all which a considerate person may hope to get for himself from howsoever high-soaring ideas or from anything else incidental to human living. Meanwhile, if he be a poet—of the school of Marlowe, say, as John Charteris interprets this poet—he will endeavor, even upon Walburga's Eve, to create something more durable and more important than is human living.

IN REVISING the text of *Beyond Life* I now and then observed the orotundity of John Charteris, deeming it disastrously Southern. I uplifted a critical eyebrow or two over so much rhetoric thus rather indiscriminately mingled with unabashed colloquialisms. I noted the pariah words, the outcast phrases, unlicensed by the Oxford English Dictionary as that august compilation was not—after all—handed down from Sinai. And yet, upon the whole, I left unamended most of these peccadilloes. I left them unchastened and unformalized, upon the perhaps inadequate ground that such actually is the fashion in which John Charteris talked. Well primed, if not exactly tipsy, with the home brew of his own garrulity, he may seem now and then to flounder, and sometimes to stumble outright, in the tumultuous, too quick advance of his argument: he very certainly upon many occasions leaps from the paved ways of logical rectitude in order to pirouette among whatsoever flowers of fancy may blossom in the by-lying meadows of irrelevance.

Far more trying to me in my rôle as editor did I over and yet over again find the fact that, in the main, John Charteris speaks—as another typewriter than mine has declared,—"in that hesitating and hair-splitting manner of men seeking the last refinement of truth, full of reservations and qualifications and after-thoughts (the foot-notes all included in the text, as De Quincey rather suggests they should be), and with every grade of subordination duly recorded in the flexible medium of adverbial modifiers."

That with a vengeance I found to be true of John

Charteris as he talks in *Beyond Life*. The sentence
and the complete thought stay always his units: even
when his ardors kindle (as when, for an instance, he
speaks of Mrs. Millamant) he yet labors to compel
each sentence and each thought, with its every least
side-light, to correspond without any surplus or re-
trenchment, at the high cost of requiring the minds
of his hearers to remain continuously alert. Readers
do not delight in any such requirement, I reflected
thriftily; nor does such conscientious writing repay
its publishers.

Well, and it might, of course, be possible for me
to prune. I might compress and trim the tale of this
verbal outing into a form which would be super-
ficially more definite and more instantly incisive, and
more indulgent to every reader's native indolence,—
into a form, in brief, which would be very much
easier reading. Yet here arose no sensible need, I
decided, to put into quite definite form the indefinite,
or to make easy reading of the undeciphered. For the
upshot of so much divagation and rhetorical em-
broidery and guess-work is, after all: "To what does
the whole business of our human living tend?—Why,
but how, in heaven's name, should I know!"

That verdict, and the ill-regulated but not ever
long-faced approach thereto which is made by John
Charteris, appeared to me when I re-wrote *Beyond
Life* to strike the key note of the Biography nicely

enough. So I let the far-wandering mannerisms of it all stand, after some casual tidying.

YET this Charteris speaks from a perished world, he babbles, to our semi-paralyzed anarchy, of a civilization as firm-rooted as was Babylon's and as similarly remote nowadays. Upon the Walburga's Eve of 1918, for example, Prohibition, which seems in particular to have fretted John Charteris, was an unavoidable experiment rather than an accomplished disaster from which human morals have not yet recovered and possibly may not ever recover. Yet another experiment equally noble in purpose, in the form of an heroic war to protect our pocket-books, was then going on in Europe, with some incidental uncharitableness being manifested by the enemy; but we were at least spared the virulent hatred of our allies. Col. Theodore Roosevelt still lived; and the fact that Col. William Jennings Bryan was dead remained as yet undetected by Col. Bryan. With that accuracy which befits a schoolteacher, Dr. Woodrow Wilson was filling the former station of Major William McKinley and of Hon. James K. Polk; and in a great many quarters was being taken quite as seriously as had been his predecessors during their own personally directed homicides upon a large scale, for moral principles so consistently elevated that they have never yet sunk into human comprehension. In 1918 not even the most earnest-minded woman was allowed to vote and thus to cleanse American politics of all corruption.

Upon the Walburga's Eve of 1918 the novels of Miss Marie Corelli and the critical pronouncements of Professor William Lyon Phelps yet kept incredible the world of polite letters: and William Dean Howells also was moribund only in his artistic standing. Many—*quorum*, as the learned phrase it, *pars fui*—cherished fond hopes as to Mr. Booth Tarkington's literary future. Mr. Robert W. Chambers had been duly elected a member of the National Institute of Arts and Letters. It was still possible to regard the comedies of William Congreve as more indelicate than the current stage attractions. In moving pictures all shades of disapproval were expressed by throwing a custard pie. Of these unbelievable phenomena does John Charteris speak, just in passing, as mere truisms. Yes, beyond any doubt, the Walburga's Eve of 1918 is removed from us by more than the passing of years or by time's normal nibbling at the accepted large verities of life.

Yet, upon the whole, I find the dicta of John Charteris to be cogent enough to-day. He speaks, I admit, not the whole truth as to Marlowe and Congreve and Nicolas de Caen and Villon and Sheridan and Dickens and Dr. Harold Bell Wright and still other persons: but I fail to detect him in an absolute misstatement. It stays of course the inescapable defect of any such cursory summing up, in a few hundred words, of any person's life and accomplishment, that of necessity so much is left out. What remains is, thus, always a little too free of qualification; it lacks the urbanity of nuance; and it tends to present as a real human being a sketch, howsoever spirited, done in primary colors.

Occasionally, I grant you, Charteris leaves out something of actual importance. I recall, for example, that in speaking of Christopher Marlowe he showed me, in that far-off April of 1918, among his collection of unwritten books, the pamphlet in which Mr. J. Leslie Hotson had not yet recorded the findings of the coroner's jury at the Deptford Strand inquest held on 1 June 1593, "*super visum Cristoferi Morley ibidem iacentis mortui & interfecti*," when these sixteen representative shopkeepers composed stolidly the last stanza in the bodily living of Christopher Marlowe.

It is not easy to imagine the temptation which I then resisted. This matter very strongly and very directly fortified that part of John Charteris' argument which admires the Economist. Here lay the proof—the one assured fact, indeed, among a deal of unplausible lying under oath—that Marlowe had spent actually the entire last day of his bodily living in low pot-house dissipation. Nevertheless was it, at the time when I wrote *Beyond Life*, a proof tantalisingly forbidden me to cite. You will see at once, I think, that pending the appearance of Mr. Hotson's book about a discovery which he had not yet made, no one of his not yet unearthed facts could honorably be included in any published discourse by John Charteris. For this reason, among other reasons, was all mention of this inquest omitted from *Beyond Life.*

Of another matter I would speak more guardedly. In what Charteris says as to the Witch-Woman the generality will find a mere re-hashing of old-fangled odds and stale ends of folk-lore. A few will recognize that Charteris was here playing with unspeakably dangerous material, in bland unconsciousness of its real nature. His hurtless becks and nods concerning "Rosicrucians," and his air-light consideration of "sorcery"—as Charteris misnamed that which only the ignorant would attempt to name at all—I still find to be diverting enough, as a rhetorical exercise. The rather horrible truth which underlies these paragraphs—the truth which, very certainly, was not ever apparent to Charteris—will be detected only by the few to whom it now can do no harm.

Beyond Life owes so much to Guy Holt that it could hardly have been dedicated to anybody else. A large deal of this book was stumbled upon in talk with

him, during the first four years or so that this the
most cordial and efficient of friends, and the most
helpful of literary editors whom any author has ever
had, was quite fruitlessly attempting to sell my books,
and—with an obstinacy at which I now marvel for
an embarrassing variety of reasons—was none the
less insistent upon publishing yet more of them.
Then, too, the stumbling was done by both of us.
Whole paragraphs of *Beyond Life*, in fact ——

But upon second thought I leave the confession
aposiopetic. Precisely how much Guy Holt has contributed to the pages of *Beyond Life*, alike in the
way of notions and of phraseology, I in self-protec-
tion shall not attempt to declare. As to several of
my other books, indeed, but through exactly the same
motives of vain-glory, I shall always exercise the
same reticence: and looking back upon our twelve-
year-long association, I gratefully recognize that no
author was ever more lucky in his publisher, through
standards not merely material. It thus appears
through the most happy of accidents that the first
in official ranking of those books which compose the
Biography of the Life of Manuel should be in-
scribed to that person to whom my indebtedness as
a writer is paramount.

Beyond Life was begun in 1917; and it received its
final touches at Virginia Beach during the atro-

ciously hot August of 1918, at a season when the
daily temperature, ranging around a hundred and
fifteen degrees, was not favorable to rhetoric. Space
does not serve to explain how much matter not
originally designed to figure in the pages of *Beyond
Life* was fitted ultimately into the hospitable form
of this volume.

During the spring and summer months of 1918 a
considerable part of *Beyond Life* was run serially
by Burton Rascoe in the literary page of the *Chicago Tribune*; and it thus evoked in Chicago, among
the indigenous literati, a lively and a largely as-
persive amount of discussion. The debate, though,
as to the most probable cause of my weak-minded-
ness, stayed regrettably local. And by-and-by *Beyond
Life* was published in book form, in the January of
1919.

Beyond Life was the first of my books to be at all
extensively reviewed: and the reviews tended, as a
whole, to belittle me under gratifyingly larger head
lines than I had thitherto been accorded. This fact,
however, had no detectable effect upon the sales of
Beyond Life, which did not—so near as I now recall
—pass 3000 during the first year of the book's existence.

Yet for a collection of essays really to "sell" we
had never esteemed humanly possible; and we had
perforce published *Beyond Life* as a collection of
essays, because of everybody's inability to contrive

a more accurate description. Perhaps the book is really a collection of essays. But I think it is not. I think that *Beyond Life* ought to be regarded as one single and one tolerably coherent essay, which is—in the author's intention, at least—a Prologue to the Biography of the Life of Manuel, not only as that life was lived by him, but also as that life was perpetuated in his children, and through the descendants of these children, down to our present time.

The Lineage of Lichfield

YOU have in *The Lineage of Lichfield* that book
which Lewis Galantière once desired me to
make, in just the utterly unreadable form which he
at the time suggested. I regret that in no less devas-
tating manner could I well dispose of the question
which Galantière then raised, a bit sceptically, as to
"the connecting theme" of my books in gross.

The quite obvious connection is the fact that they
constitute a huge family tree, which in *The Lineage
of Lichfield* I have presented at full length, for the
confusion of anybody's attempt to read it. These
twenty books form a genealogy—although for reasons that are hereinafter made plain, the compiler
elects to call it a Biography—of which the evolution
was begun as far back as 1901, when I wrote, in
Love-Letters of Falstaff, the first of the stories
afterward bound up together as *The Line of Love*.
And the general "method" followed in that volume
—of depicting a decisive passage in the lives of two
persons of opposite sex, then a similar untying of
knots in the life of a child of that couple, and yet

afterward in one of the grandchildren's heart-history—has been extended, but never altered, in my succeeding volumes. The most plain connection of the various books included in the Biography is, thus, precisely the same connection that exists between the several stories in my first written book, *The Line of Love*. And all traces from Dom Manuel, through the descendants whom he and Alianora left in England, and through the other descendants whom he and Niafer left in Poictesme, and through the eleven images that he and Freydis informed with fire from Audela and set to live as abnormal men among normal mankind.

Yet I elect to think that, in a deeper sense, the coherency of these books is not merely genealogic. *Beyond Life* now stands as a sort of preface, to embody the vital and æsthetic theories thereafter builded on, as well as generally to indicate the forces to which my protagonist later reacts and the three codes by which, at one or another time, he is swayed. Forthwith, in *Figures of Earth* and in *The Silver Stallion*, you have Manuel posed as the ancestor and the life-source of all my leading characters; as by-and-by, after the theme of chivalry has been more or less disposed of, Jurgen enters the Biography in a similar rôle. Forthwith, too, you have my protagonist. For it is the life of Manuel, and the life of Jurgen, as this life is perpetuated in the descendants of both, that I continue to tell about. The vital

principle of each of these extreme types is presently
blended with the other, in the person and in the
progeny of Mélite de Puysange; and the compound
—need one say?—is very variously affected and
guided and foiled by the milieu in which it thereafter
happens to find itself. But with Manuel's life, so
oddly changed now by its mixing with Jurgen's life,
as the compound is transmitted, through a score-
and-odd of generations, down to the present continuance of its thriving in Lichfield—with this
protagonist are my books concerned always.

Manuel, let me say here, I planned to be the type
which finds its sole, if incomplete, expression in action: I have, in consequence, been at some trouble
to refrain from ascribing to Dom Manuel any
thoughts whatsoever. And Jurgen was designed to
illustrate Dom Manuel's utmost contrary, in that
Jurgen derives his real, his deepest, his one unfailing
pleasure from the exercise, not of that member with
which his name has been associated most often by
the more prurient, but of his mind. To Jurgen, the
progenitor of all the gallant people, of all the poets,
and of all the inadequate, unpractical persons in
general to be found in my books, the most interesting thing in this not incessantly interesting world—
in fact, the one wholly worth-while avocation—is to
watch his own brain at work, especially when this
fine and curious toy is set to outmatch the working
of some other brain . . . Between these two ex-

tremes range the inherited traits of their descendants, who display, in so far as my art could manage
this, an occasional family resemblance. And the
"connecting theme" of my books, viewed in this light,
would seem to be the lean and dusty axiom that human beings are pretty much the same in most times
and stations, and come by varying roads, as did
Jurgen the pawnbroker and Manuel the high Count,
to pretty much the same end. They suggest, in brief,
that life is remarkably repetitious.

Yet, underlying all, is the quite other "connecting
theme," that Horvendile may be an erratic demiurge
who composes and controls the entire business ex-
tempore, without any prompter except his own
æsthetic whims: but that is really a matter almost
too complex here to explain. Rather does discretion
urge me to refer you to Sævius Nicanor's fine chapter on this very interesting theory. For it all comes
back to theory, and to the cooling reflection that it
is the nature of every explanatory theory to be
evolved some while after the phenomena which it
accounts for,—even, I suspect, when it is one's own
theory about one's own books.

IN ANY event, it was the suggestion of Lewis Galantière, as made to me late in 1920, that I should com-
pile and put in order such a selection from Colonel
Rudolph Musgrave's books and from his various

genealogical notes and articles (now enriching oc-
cultly the back files of the *Lichfield Historical Association's Quarterly Magazine*) as would make plain
the family connection between my chronicles of Lichfield and the stories of Poictesme. In *The Lineage
of Lichfield* is that selection. In *The Lineage of
Lichfield* that relationship is set forth, simply and
baldly, with no effort toward any of the auctorial
graces save the lean virtue of clarity. Just to be
clear, is my one aim: and so I need not tell you that
in *The Lineage of Lichfield* I avoid all pedantry and
shun the antiquary's dark vice of larding his clipped
jargon with as many tatters of strange tongues and
of patriarchal spelling as he can possibly lug in
anywhere that plain English would serve him better.

Now on the face of it, *The Lineage of Lichfield*
is a pedigree which indicates the descent of various
persons, about whom I have written a great number
of books and short stories, from Dom Manuel of
Poictesme. In reality, I think, this volume is an outline—or, say, a map—of some nine centuries of Dom
Manuel's life, the life of which my other books are
the Biography. For, be it repeated, the life that informed tall Manuel the Redeemer did not become
extinct when the old champion rode westward with
Grandfather Death. The body and the appearance
of Dom Manuel had gone. But his life remained
perpetuated in divers children—in, to be accurate, a
respectable total of sixteen persons,—who afterward

transmitted this life to their progeny, as did they in turn to their own offspring. So this life flowed on through time—and through such happenings in France and England and America as, one by one, my books have recorded,—with every generation dividing and subdividing the troubled and attritioned flowing into more numerous streamlets. And Manuel's life came thus to Lichfield, by-and-by, and is not yet extinct in my contemporary Townsends and Kennastons and Musgraves, of all whom in *The Lineage of Lichfield* I trace out the descent from Manuel.

It is about this life that I have written in many places, in the various chapters of a Biography which runs nowadays to a quite imposing number of volumes, but stays incomplete, and cannot ever be completed, in any true sense, by mortal hands. This life of Manuel, as I write about it, appears to me a stream that, in journeying toward an unpredictable river, which is itself the tributary of an unplumbed ocean, is fretted at random (still to preserve the fluvial analogue) by the winds of time and by many pebbles of chance. It is, like that brook in the gardens of Storisende over which Dame Melicent philosophized in her old age, forever unchanged as a whole, and yet forever changing in all its parts. Time and chance affect it continually. So are there various ripples raised upon the stream as it goes—ultimately —seaward: and, noting these, we say this ripple is

Manuel, that Ormskirk, and the other Charteris;
noting also that while we name it the small lively
stirring is gone. But the stream remains unabated;
nor is the sureness of its moving lessened, any more
than is the obscurity of its origin and of its goal.

OR LET us shift the figure. Let us, rather, liken this
continuously re-incarnated life of Manuel to an
itinerant comedian that with each generation assumes the garb of a new body, and upon a new stage
enacts a variant of yesterday's drama. For I do not
find the comedy ever to be much altered in its essentials. I incline hereabouts to side with those more
acute critics who—pending their discovery that the
Atlantic ocean is damp and the moon shiny—have
discovered the Biography to be "repetitious." I incline to accept, in brief, that same summary of each
human life which Horvendile delivered to Florian
de Puysange beside the asherah stone. The first act
is the imagining of a place where contentment exists
and may be come to; and the second act reveals the
striving toward, and the third act the falling short
of, that shining goal, or else (the difference here
being negligible) the attaining of it,—to discover
that happiness, after all, abides a thought farther
down the bogged, rocky, clogged, befogged heart-
breaking road, if anywhere. That is the comedy
which, to my finding, the life of Manuel has en-

acted over and yet over again upon every stage between Poictesme and Lichfield. That is the comedy
upon which, over and yet over again, the last curtain
has been lowered by Grandfather Death.

I call it "a comedy." Really there is thin sus-
tenance for the tragic muse in the fact that with
each performance the flesh-and-blood costume of
the protagonist is spoiled, and the human body temporarily informed with Manuel's life is thrown perforce to the dust-heap. There is not even apparent
to reflection any economic loss. For the wardrobe of
this world-roving vagabond is self-replenishing, in
that as each costume is used, it thriftily begets new
apparel for the comedian to ruin in to-morrow's
rendering of the old play. The parent's flesh is flung
by, like an outworn coat: but the comedian—reclad
with the child's body, tricked out with strong fresh
sinews, re-rouged with youth, and fortified with a
young heart—he is lustily refurbishing, through a
garnish of up-to-date local allusions and of the very
latest social and religious and political catchwords,
all the archaic dialogue and the inveterate "situations" of yesterday's hackneyed performance.

NOW, in the light of this comedic metaphor—the
metaphor which upon the whole I prefer—the Biography can deal with no large portion of the vagabond's wardrobe. The Biography has concerned it-

self with only that relatively brief part of the tour wherein life has worn human bodies. Previously, they report, the scenery was arboreal, and our comedian wore fur and a tail; as before that, his costume was reptilian, and yet earlier, was piscine. So do the scientists trace backward his career, to life's first appearance upon any terrestrial stage, when the *vis comica* which later was to animate the thews of Manuel had for its unassuming apparel only a small single bubble stuck in primeval slime.

Well, and since that modest début our comedian has dressed his rôle with an always increasing elaborateness, in the while that he progressed from a mere pinhead of sentiency toward all the intricate fripperies of the human body, with its wealth of modern improvements, in the form of forward-looking bifocal eyes, and of prehensile fingers, and of lips which are alike kissable and multiloquent, and of that last word in mammalian luxury, a vermiform appendix which supports surgeons. Nor is this the total of his advancement and of his endless inventings. So magnificently, through many centuries of endeavor, has he reorganized his stage-settings also, in the more favored nooks of Earth which he has enriched with his main centres of civilization and with his stupendous fulminating wars, that it is not past the reach of poetic imagining to suppose the telescopes of Earth's nearer neighbors may quite possibly have detected some one of these fermenting pustules. Upon Mars, perhaps, these phenomena have been noticed by the philosophers of that planet: they have deduced, it may be, that our comedian exists; and at this same instant they may be wondering what on Earth he is up to.

That proud contingency, I admit, remains guesswork; but it is certain that less remotely this comedian has made sure of his art's final need. Upon Earth's epidermis, I mean, he has created his own audience, making it more indisputable and more immediate than are those possibly perturbed Martians, by training some cells in the human brain every once and a while to think. And I infer that, since every form of æsthetic endeavor is spurred nobly by any prospect of applause from any source howsoever trivial, the performance may well be given nowadays with a renewed gusto, now that the comedian's antics needs be marvelled over by this gray beading so unobtrusively inwrought into his most recent costume.

Yet is there a drawback to this evolving of man's brain as a dramatic critic. This drawback is, that the one honest verdict to be wrung from the small wet sponge which lines all skulls, informing even the crania of many authors and of admired clergymen, must be a lament that, at its every performance, the play has been confined a bit too depressingly to this theme of striving toward a goal which, no matter whether it is gained or lost, proves not to be the

desired goal. And then *da capo*. Yes, it really is depressing, because there is, in this unending captaincy
of a forlorn hope, and in the futile and obstinate
romanticism of life's vaudeville, just that high-
hearted quality to which all our better-thought-of
"realists" most strenuously object, as being "untrue
to life"; and in the withering light of our best
æsthetic theories, the performance seems wanly
rococo and unreal.

I SHALL not speak here of the future, before which,
in point of fact, my imaginings balk. To-morrow the
age-old comedian will be doing and wearing none
knows what, although in reason the experimental
artist that we call "life" cannot stay forever content with human bodies for his apparel and medium.
Already, in considerate eyes, life tends to some more
handsome expression, by means of the harnessed
chemistries, the caged explosions, the collaborating
fly-wheels and vapors and wire-dancing thunderbolts,
that in all our cities bedwarf the human beings who
serve mainly as release levers. Already, as a great
many philosophers have recognised, we are so generally fed and clothed and sheltered and carried
everywhither by machinery that we can lay no grave
claim to be thought more than its parasites. And
already the era appears well in sight when every
need of civilization and of its victims will be dis-

charged by the pressure of electric buttons, so that, in America at least, the one essential part of man will be his fore-finger.

But at prophecy, I repeat, I balk. I was once tempted to weigh the likelihood that, with disuse, the other members and organs in general of mankind would atrophy and would disappear; and that our national nicety would then make an end of all by suppressing this surviving lone fore-finger, as a probably phallic symbol. Since then we have become a wide deal less prudish; we bid fair to attend to our racial suicide in a rather different manner; and at all events here is no need for me to enter into these high considerations. It may seem to hide-bound logic quite certain that human beings are just one season's fashion in life's clothes, and that next season something entirely different will be worn. With such sartorial forecasts I have in this place no quarrel; and if I do not tell you the real truth of the matter it is merely because I do not know this truth. I merely know that, even though the life of our planet may by-and-by discard mankind just as it has discarded the dodo and the dinosaur, yet at present mere men and mere women are life's latest clothing: and I take it to be the part of urbanity to accept the mode of one's day. So must I tacitly confine myself to the anthropologic season in Dom Manuel's endlessly world-roving life without venturing to prattle about apotheoses.

I ADD here, as a matter of slight factual interest, that *The Lineage of Lichfield* was written in the summer of 1921, especially for what I imagine to have been the most easily indescribable of all American magazines, the *Reviewer*. The *Reviewer*, as published at Richmond-in-Virginia—from a side alley, in immediate antagonism to a cathedral—was at this season in theory a fortnightly periodical, which in point of fact appeared whensoever the editors thought it might perhaps be amusing to get out another issue. In any case, the *Reviewer* was scheduled to become a monthly magazine in the autumn of 1921, and I had agreed to edit the first three issues in this new avatar. I did edit them, to such an extent as the vagaries of the printer permitted: and *The Lineage of Lichfield* thus made its tri-partite appearance, in the October, November and December numbers, for 1921, of the *Reviewer*. It was largely due to this fact, my conscience now and then tells me, that the *Reviewer* was not long afterward forced to become a quarterly, and by-and-by a legend.

Figures of Earth

*F*IGURES OF EARTH is, with some superficial air of paradox, the one volume in the long Biography of the Life of Manuel which deals with the lifetime of Dom Manuel. Most of the matter strictly appropriate to a Preface you may find, if you so elect, in the Foreword addressed to Sinclair Lewis. And in fact, after writing two prefaces to introduce *Figures of Earth*—first, in this epistle to Lewis, and secondly, in the remarks added to the illustrated edition in 1925—I had thought this volume could very well continue to survive, for so long as its deficiencies permit, without the confection of a third preface, until I began a little more carefully to consider this romance, in the seventh year of its existence, when I rewrote *Figures of Earth* for the Storisende edition.

Well, and I then noted that its deficiency in chief (like the superior officer of a disastrously wrecked crew) lay in the fact that what I had meant to be the main "point" of *Figures of Earth*, while explicitly enough stated in the book, remains for every practical end indiscernible. . . . I have written I do not remember how many books during the last I prefer to forget how many years. Yet of these books —as I do remember, with a strange clearness—this is the single book which began at one plainly recognizable instant with one plainly recognizable imagining. It is the only book by me which ever came into being, with its goal set, and with its theme and its contents more or less pre-determined throughout, between two ticks of the clock.

Egotism here becomes so quite unavoidable as to make happy the circumstance that the intelligent do not mislike egotism, that font of fine literature. At Dumbarton Grange the library in which I wrote for some twelve years, between 1913 and 1926, was lighted by three windows set side by side and opening outward. It was in the instant of unclosing the most westerly of these windows, on a sunlit afternoon in the April of 1919, to speak with a woman and a child who were then returning to the house (with the day's batch of mail from the post office) that, for no reason at all, I reflected it would be regrettable if, as the moving window unclosed, that special woman and that particular child should prove to be figures in the glass, and the window should open upon nothingness. For that, I believed, was about to happen. There would be revealed, I knew, beyond that now moving window, when it had opened all the way, not absolute darkness, but a

gray nothingness, rather sweetly scented . . . Well!
there was not. I once more enjoyed the normal, the
quite familiar experience of being mistaken. I record
gratefully that nothing whatever came of that panic
surmise, of that second-long nightmare—of that
brief but over-tropical flowering of indigestion, it
may have been—except at long last the 80,000 words
or so of *Figures of Earth*.

I WAS already planning to begin on "the book about
Manuel" later in that year. His gray and generally
steel-like appearance and his nature, as a not ever
finally solved riddle, were known to me; as well as
his intimacy with Queen Alianora and with Queen
Freydis (who as yet had no name), and the fact
that he was married to some other woman. I had
learned, from my other romances, who were his
children, and who had been the sole witness of his
death, inasmuch as I had read about that, with
some interest, in the fourth chapter of *Jurgen*. But
I did not know what in particular had happened to
him.

Now, though, I had the gist of "the book about
Manuel"—in the instant, in that lonely and quiet
moment, when Dom Manuel opens a window, in his
own somewhat over-familiar home, to see his wife
and his child, his lands, and all the Poictesme of

which he was at once the master and the main glory, presented as bright, shallow, very fondly loved illusions in the protective glass of Ageus. I knew that the all-horrible thing which had not happened to me—nor, I hope, to anybody—was precisely the thing, and the most important thing, which had happened to the gray Count of Poictesme.

So that evening I made a brief memorandum of this historical circumstance. For a month or two *Figures of Earth* existed only in the form of that memorandum. Then, through as it were this window, I began to grope at "the book about Manuel," and from the unclosing of this window I developed *Figures of Earth*, necessarily for the most part toward anterior events. For it seemed to me—as it still seems—that the opening of this particular magic casement, upon an outlook rather more perilous and heart-disturbing than the bright foam of faëry seas, was alike the climax and the main "point" of my book.

Yet this fact, I am resignedly sure, as I nowadays appraise this romance, could not ever be detected by any conceivable reader of *Figures of Earth*. In consequence, it has been thought well here to confess at some length the original conception of this volume, without at all going into the value of that conception, nor into, heaven knows, how this conception came thus successfully to be obscured by its author.

so I began "the book about Manuel" that summer
—in 1919, upon the back porch of our cottage at
the Rockbridge Alum Springs, whence, as I recall
it, one could always, just as Manuel did upon Upper
Morven, regard the changing green and purple of
the mountains and the tall clouds trailing northward,
and could observe that the sunlit splendors one
viewed were all gigantic and lovely and seemed not to
be very greatly bothering about humankind. I suppose, though, that in point of fact it occasionally
rained. In any case, upon that same porch, as it
happened, this book was finished rather more than
a year afterward, in the August of 1920.

The notes made at this time, preparatory to writing *Figures of Earth*, reveal much which nowadays
has become incomprehensible. There was once an
Olrun in the book; and I can recollect how her part
in the story was absorbed by two of the other characters—by Suskind and by Alianora. Freydis, it appears, was originally called Hlif. Miramon at one
stage in the book's being, I find with real surprise,
was married *en secondes noces* to Math. Othmar has
lost that pre-eminence which once was his. And it
seems, too, there once figured in Manuel's heart affairs a Bel-Imperia, who, so near as I can deduce
from my notes, was a lady in a tapestry, to whom
magic lent flesh and accessibility. Someone un-
stitched her, ruinously; and yet her destruction was
only partial, for I suspect that a few skeins of this

otherwise forgotten Bel-Imperia endure in the Rade-
gonde of *Straws and Prayer-Books*, whereas the
name of Bel-Imperia also has been preserved in another story.

Nor can I make anything whatever out of my
notes about Guivret (who seems to have been in
no way connected with Guivric the Sage), nor about
Biduz, nor about the Anti-Pope—even though, to be
sure, one mention of this heresiarch does yet survive in the present text of *Figures of Earth*. I am
wholly baffled to read, in my own penciling, such
proposed chapter headings as "The Jealousy of
Niafer" and "How Sclaug Loosed the Dead"—
which latter memorandum is dyed yet deeplier with
the incomprehensible through being annotated
"(?Phorgemon)". I do not know anything about
Phorgemon nowadays. Moreover, "The Spirit Who
Had Half of Everything," in addition to a whole
chapter about himself as I once planned *Figures of
Earth*, seems to have been exorcised pretty thoroughly . . . No; I find a great many of my old
notes as to this book merely bewildering; and I find,
too, something of pathos in these embryons of un-
born day-dreams which, for this cause or the other,
were obliterated, and which have been utterly forgotten by their creator, very much as in this book
vexed Miramon Lluagor twists off the head of a not
quite satisfactory, whimpering design, and drops the
valueless fragments into his waste-basket. . . . But

I do know that the entire book developed, howsoever helter-skelter, and after fumbling in no matter how many blind alleys, from that first memorandum about the troubling window of Ageus. All
leads toward—and through—that window.

THE book, then, was published in the February of
1921. I need not here deal with its semi-serial appearance in the guise of short stories: these details
are recorded in another place. But I confess, with
appropriate humility, that the reception of *Figures
of Earth* by the reading public was a depressing
business. This romance, at that time, through one
extraneous reason and another, disappointed well-
nigh everybody, for all that it has since become, so
near as I can judge, the best liked of my books,
especially among women. It seems, indeed, a fact
sufficiently edifying that, in appraising the two leg-
endary heroes of Poictesme, the sex of whom Jurgen esteemed himself a connoisseur should almost
unanimously prefer Manuel.
    For the rest, this *Figures of Earth* appeared im-
mediately following, and during the temporary se-
questration of, *Jurgen*. The fact was forthwith discovered, quite unreticently, that in *Figures of Earth*
I had not succeeded in an attempt to rewrite its
predecessor: and my crass failure to do this, a failure so open, so flagrant, and so undeniable, caused

what I can only describe as the instant and over-
whelming and universal triumph of *Figures of Earth*
to be precisely what did not occur. In 1921 Com-
stockery still surged in full cry against the impris-
oned pawnbroker and the crimes of his author, both
literary and personal; and the, after all, tolerably
large portion of the reading public who were not
disgusted by Jurgen's lechery, were enraged now, so
near as I could gather, by Manuel's lack of it.

It followed in the spring of 1921 that, among
those futile persons who use serious, long words in
talking about mere books, some aggrieved reproof
of my auctorial malversations, upon the one ground
or the other, became biloquial and pandemic. Nor
was that the sum of this book's harsh weird: not
many other volumes, I believe, have been burlesqued
and cried down in print by their own dedicatees.
. . . But from the cicatrix of that time-healed
wound I turn away. I preserve a forgiving silence,
comparable to that of Hermione in the fifth act of
A Winter's Tale. I resolve that when I mention the
names of Louis Untermeyer and H. L. Mencken
it shall always be in some connection more pleasant,
and that here I shall avoid mention of their names.

Meanwhile from the fifteen or so experiments in
contrapuntal prose I remained unique in deriving
pleasure, where others found bewilderment and no
tongue-tied irritation. They inferred, quite sensibly,
that I was up to something which I would not be

keeping thus dark if its nature were praiseworthy. But in general, and above every misdemeanor else, the book fretted everybody by not being a more successfully managed re-hashing of the then notorious *Jurgen.*

Since 1921, and since the rehabilitation of *Jurgen,* the notion has uprisen, gradually, among the more bold and speculative thinkers, that perhaps, after all, I was not attempting, in this *Figures of Earth,* to re-hash *Jurgen*; and Manuel has made his own friends. I must add, however, that at no time since 1921 have I published a book which was not disposed of, with the same unanimity, in the light of the book's likeness to, and of its differences from, *Jurgen.*

Well, and I would not appear boastful. Yet, inasmuch as my advisers have been so helpful as to point out, upon certainly not less than a thousand occasions, that any likeness proves the decay of my powers through this lapse into self-imitation, and that any difference proves the decay of my powers by the revealed inability to regain earlier levels, I really have weighed carefully, I think, all this fifteen-year-long adhortation, with the respect due to its helpfulness.

The Silver Stallion

WITH *The Silver Stallion* the Biography turns to those who in some sense were—just as Jurgen asserts—"Dom Manuel's children in the spirit." Yet upon that relationship, as actually familiary, I would not insist. Rather was it my aim in this book to record the growth of the great legend of Manuel as a spiritual Redeemer; and in particular to trace the slowly widening influence of this legend among those persons who had known Manuel almost intimately. I agree with Freydis that, for various reasons, nobody ever did know Manuel really well.

The protagonist of *The Silver Stallion* is, thus, if not truly Manuel himself, yet an idea about Manuel,—an idea presented at the moment of its conception, and thence passing through its infancy and its little regarded youth, unhurt by the ragings of Coth or by the unregeneracy of Gonfal and of Miramon, to come gradually to full growth and vigor; until at the end of the book this idea, which stays always the book's hero, is dismissed, in accord-

ance with the true romantic code, to live happily
ever afterward, in the heart of Donander Veratyr.
I mean, of course, the idea that Manuel, who yesterday had been the physical Redeemer of Poictesme, would by-and-by return as his people's spiritual Redeemer.

It is true that this ideal protagonist of *The Silver
Stallion* did not live happily ever afterward upon a
planet not over-fertile in perpetual bliss. Instead,
for all earthly purposes, the great legend of Manuel
was definitely annihilated during the fourteenth century by Manuel's reputed great-grandson: but with
that fact we have in *The Silver Stallion* no concern.

OUR concern here is with the fact that, if the annals
of Poictesme are to be trusted, Dom Manuel for a
long while flourished quite handsomely as a messiah.
He had his vogue and his enthusiasts, without ever
having much else in common with those hordes of
pagan Redeemers who, at odd times, have brought
the consolations and ferocities of religion to innumerable millions. There was the plain difference, to
begin with, that Dom Manuel was worshipped by
staunch Christians.

We forget now and then that this faith in a returning messiah is from the Christian standpoint
not of necessity an heretical doctrine. Piety has
looked for the return of many Redeemers less

heathenish than was Hammurabi or Krishna or Saoshyant; not merely Bar-Kokebas and Moses of Crete, not only David Alroy and Sabbatai Sevi, have been revealed, through the direct intervention of Heaven, as the one true Savior's incarnation in human flesh; Popé and Teuskwa'tawa also have had their compeers in a more civilized form of worship; and the Mahdis, the countless scores of Mahdis since the days of Mohammed Ibn al Hanafiyah— all those divinely inspired Redeemers whose coming has so frequently justified the faith of Islam—have yet been less numerous than the Redeemers who were gratifyingly untainted by paganism. And among this latter class of Redeemers, of course, should be ranked Dom Manuel.

Hereabouts, then, it is needful to bear in mind that this belief in a Redeemer who is to return to-morrow attended by every nature of supernal splendor, is not merely a heathen superstition; and that some such tenet has been found, time and again, to be wholly consistent with continued membership in this or the other branch of the Christian church. Dom Manuel we may thus assume to have been worshipped unrecusantly, well within the confines of the Christian faith, very much as Elkesai was once worshipped by a division of the Ebionites, and St. James the Just by the Eucharists, and Hans Böhm by the Taborites, and John of Leyden by the Ana-baptists. Dom Manuel, let us say, was for a while

as ardently believed, by the most zealous sort of
Christians, to be mankind's predestined spiritual Redeemer as, for a while also, was Venner the Wine
Cooper—or as was Anne Lee, or as was Savely
Kapustin, or as was (to a necessarily more limited
extent) that divine son of Joanna Southcott who
vexatiously failed to be born. Dom Manuel, in fine,
according to the annals of Poictesme, was worshipped without any paganism, as a purely Christian
messiah, just as at yet other times and in other lands
were worshipped Melchoir Hoffman and Arise Evans
and Danelo Filopovitch and John Alexander Dowie.

To-day, of course, no one of these Christian Redeemers is at all honored, unless the Doukhobors
still await the return of Kapustin. I am sure I do not
know. But each Christian messiah had once a vogue,
and a formally organized and endowed church
wherein to be worshipped, and had enthusiasts who
endured persecution for his sake, and who died under
torment for his sake—or, it might be, for her sake—
very gladly. Each had his day; and each, within a
howsoever unenormous circle of adherents, awakened a sustaining faith, which appears to be vitally
necessary for most men's contentment, in this age-
old legend of the all-powerful Redeemer who will
come again, to-morrow.

The theme of *The Silver Stallion*, then, is how this
legend came to attach itself to Dom Manuel; how,
in particular, this legend afterward affected, or failed

to affect suitably, those persons who had known Dom
Manuel with some intimateness; and how in the end
nobody believed in this legend any longer except
Donander Veratyr. But Donander Veratyr was God.
You should remember that fact.

The Silver Stallion was planned more or less completely while I was finishing *Figures of Earth,* in
1920. Two of the episodes, dealing severally with
the footprints of Ninzian and with Toupan's bright
bees, were written early in 1922; but not until the
autumn of 1924 was the book begun formally. It
was finished in the September of 1925: and I may
here record that the exodus from out of my keeping
of the sole existing complete copy of *The Silver
Stallion* was then haunted on the one side by tragedy
and on the other by somewhat miraculously good
luck.

My typescript was mailed at Dumbarton. Now at
Dumbarton, I must explain, the outgoing mail-bag is
hanged on a sort of gibbet beside the railway track;
and as the mail train thunders by, it disdainfully
acquires this mail-bag with a large iron hook. I have
observed the performance many hundred times; and
always I was moved by its petulance. No mail train
ever seemed to convey any of my work toward publication except with frank and gigantic distaste.

On that special day perhaps this distaste became

active rebellion. At all events, when the typescript
of *The Silver Stallion* was mailed, late on a Saturday
afternoon, then the viciously lunging huge hook
struck just a little too low. It thus ripped open the
mail-bag; and, carrying off the remainder of the
mail, to the last least post card, it with invidious
distinction left the typescript of *The Silver Stallion*
lying in the narrow ditch beside the Richmond, Fred-
ericksburg and Potomac Railway. There my typescript remained all night: and, as I must here repeat,
this was then the only copy of the book anywhere
existent.

I learned slowly, through some fifteen embittered
years of experience, that no typist, without the aid
of a microscope, could decipher at all plausibly any
manuscript by me after I had once finished inter-
lining it: so I came long ago to do my own typewrit-
ing, curtailing in this way my expenditures of money
and of profanity also. I destroy that which has been
retyped, as of no further use to me; and I cannot attempt carbon copies, with any retention of equanimity, because seven times out of ten I insert the carbon
paper wrong side up. Through these causes was there
only one copy of *The Silver Stallion*; and that copy
lay overnight in a ditch.

Sunday, however, turned out to be a fine day; the
sun shone resplendently upon my now muddied,
painstakingly wrapped, quite large package; and so,

out of the scores of persons who crossed the ditch
during that forenoon, it was natural enough the very
first comer should find my typescript. As it happened,
to be sure, the parcel was not discovered by absolutely the first passer-by, nor by the second. Dozens
of people had gone by, in fact, before the hundredth
or so person to cross the railway ditch, during that
bright Sabbath, glanced casually downward, in order
to insure her foothold, and observed my three and a
half pound package not at all. Nobody ever noticed
it during the whole day. And thus *The Silver Stallion* passed yet another night out of doors, beside
the northbound track of the Richmond, Fredericks-
burg and Potomac Railway, in the mire of a ditch,
under no guardianship more immediate than the
watchfulness of Orion and of the Pleiades.

The genius of compassion whispers me not to
keep you any longer in a state of intolerable sus-
pense. Upon Monday morning, then, when the mail
carrier, after his Sabbath holiday, came to hang the
outgoing mail-bag upon the gibbet to which I have
referred, he quite unavoidably saw the package. So
it was retrieved from the ditch by Sambo Johnson
(should posterity care to applaud the name), and
found to be exceedingly soiled but unhurt. The
typescript was forwarded that Monday afternoon
to McBride's; and in due time it was published as a
book, in the April of 1926.

—ALL which constitutes no thrilling tale. My point, though, is that anybody who refuses to concede that this typescript, for at least thirty-six hours, was protected by heaven, must first presuppose, rather impiously, some supernal slackness to have been going on, for thirty-six entire hours, during any one of which ten minutes' rain would have deleted my entire year's work. My point is that this work, at the tip end of a quite showery September, did really and directly receive heaven's imprimatur; and that therefore some of the criticism which was accorded it upon publication appeared to me a little rash.

I cite, as a fair average example of this criticism, an uncommonly well-thought-of English reviewer, who was but one of that largish chorus which in 1926 thus graciously hymned the merits of *The Silver Stallion*:

"The malignity and malevolence of this monstrous literary sacrilege cannot be pardoned. Its banality is no excuse for its brutality. Its stupidity is no extenuation for its blasphemy. The author has in this book committed the unpardonable sin of art,—hooliganism. He may not be capable of understanding the vision of good that raises man above the level of vermin. He may not be able to feel the mystery of faith. He may not possess the power of reverence or the grace of humility. But he ought to love his fellow creatures, and to respect their ideals and their dreams. He may find it amusing to hurt and wound

the lowly and the simple, but he should not trample
on their highest and holiest imaginings, even if he
cannot soar out of his literary mire and mud."

Yes, howsoever much one may admire alliteration,
that does seem to me a little rash. I cannot quite
imagine heaven's protecting just that sort of book.
I concede, of course, that *The Silver Stallion* did
actually come to its publishers out of the mire and
mud of an actual Henrico County ditch. But it came
to tell (with, I think, all proper reverence) of a
legend in which most men believe instinctively, and
believe for mankind's perpetual good, even if this
legend be not true about any one of those countless
Redeemers between Hammurabi and John Alexander
Dowie,—and in the end, as I would by no means
have you not note, to dismiss this legend as yet living in the heart of that God whom men adore as
the Creator and Preserver of all earthly things.

The Witch-Woman

IT IS true I have not as yet published any book
called *The Witch-Woman.* Yet this is a delin-
quency on my part which in no way affects the fact
that after finishing *The Silver Stallion* you would do
well to read next the complete trilogy of *The Witch-
Woman,*—which consists of *The Music from Behind
the Moon,* and *The White Robe,* and *The Way of
Ecben.*

Each of these stories concerns the third daughter
of Dom Manuel and Dame Niafer, that Ettarre la
Beale of whose birth and first marriage something
has been recorded in *The Silver Stallion.* For the
rest, it is after the fashion of a prelude that this trilogy rehearses, in a narrative form but upon a sharply
limited scale, those three main themes which the
Biography is to develop, in a narrative form also,
but with more ample leisure: for this trilogy relates
how Ettarre, the all-lovely witch-woman (a personage about whom John Charteris has already told
you in *Beyond Life*) was loved by a moonstruck poet
and by a gallant bishop and by a chivalrous king.

So is it, I think, that after *The Silver Stallion*, which disposes of Manuel, ought to follow directly *The Witch-Woman*, as a sort of brief *précis* of the doings of all the oncoming descendants of Manuel.

ETTARRE, it may be recalled, was the cause of the twelve-year warring (1263-75) between her brother Count Emmerick and her lover Maugis d'Aigremont, Donander's son; and it has been told likewise how at the conclusion of this war Ettarre married Guiron des Rocques. Well, and it was her excessive beauty, they say, which provoked the continued unfriendliness of the Norns, those ageing ladies at no season pre-eminent for their beauty. At all events, it was through the Norns' decree that Ettarre was carried away from Poictesme in 1286 by Sargatanet, Lord of the Waste Behind the Moon: and it was in despite of the Norns, as you may read in the first section of this trilogy, that Ettarre was fetched back to Earth by the poet Madoc, rather early in the year 1879, about the middle of April.

Here one encounters a point somewhat abstruse and a fact not generally recognized. For you may note that, through Madoc's adroit use of punctuation, Ettarre and Madoc, upon this unexampled occasion, returned to the year of grace 1294. All that which had taken place upon Earth between 1294 and 1879 thus had to be cancelled: and everything which had happened since 1294 had to happen all over again. In brief, the entire Book of the Norns from the year 1294 onward had to be rewritten.

Now the Norns, in preparing this second version of Earth's history, which predetermined all happenings on this planet, adhered in the main to their first version, so near as they could recall it: but much slipped their memory; moreover, they introduced here and there a few ill-advised variations such as must necessarily result from the attempts of three literary ladies to revise a collaboration so exceedingly ancient that all three of them had virtually forgotten its nature and its purpose. It was simply not possible for the Norns to recapture the more richly romantic vein in which they had written, so many thousands of years earlier, at a season when, relatively speaking, they were mere chits, a good while before the Solar system had been installed in the universe: and that the Norns rather bungled the whole performance is plain to anyone who considers Earth's history in this second version, the version which is still in use on account of Madoc's meddlesomeness.

It has therefore appeared to me far better, in preparing the Biography of the Life of Manuel, to adhere to the first version of the Book of the Norns, just as I found it in the library of John Charteris. This task I have performed faithfully. It follows that the generally received history of Earth ever since the year 1294 does differ noticeably, here and there, from the first history of Earth as this history is preserved in the Biography of the Life of Manuel: but I do not think there can be any serious disputing which version is the more handsome.

THE sources of these tales appear somewhat widely various. That *The Music from Behind the Moon* is based upon the *Madoc et Ettarre* of Nicolas de Caen, is duly acknowledged in the introductory note to this story: and the tale was first put into English by me during the opening months of 1926, in a form somewhat different from that which it now displays, for the possible use of some magazine.

There was then no thought of giving it an independent publication. But when, just at this time, Guy Holt decided to leave McBride's in order to establish his own publishing firm, it seemed to me that this brief romance might not ungracefully go to my main "literary creditor" as an expression of good will toward his new venture. The story therefore was recast into its present shape, being enlarged, as I recall matters, from twenty-four chapters to thirty chapters: and a bit later, during the autumn of 1926, in an edition limited to 3000 copies, it had the honor of being the first book published by the John Day Company.

IN *The White Robe*, as completed in April 1928, and as first published by McBride's in December 1928, in an edition limited to 3290 copies, I have but attempted to render certain portions of the Life or Legend of Odo of Valnères—taking my material from the text published by the Rev. Fathers of the College of St. Hoprig, at Aigremont, in 1885 (*tom.* VI. *S. Hoprigis Opera Omnia*)—and to blend into these excerpts La Vrillière's brief account of the blessed Odo's relations with Gui de Puysange (*De Puysange et son temps*, pp. 5-7). Very little, however, except Gui's actual name, is derived from the latter source. The seventeenth century manuscript (codex 43f31 in the Vatican Library), of which the Rev. Fathers' printed legend presents its well bowdlerized version, ascribes to the old sorcerer no family name, I ought perhaps to explain; and the manuscript does not anywhere presume to mention the then powerful race of Puysange. La Vrillière, writing after the French Revolution, could afford to be bolder; and my story profits by the event.

I add merely that it was this Gui de Puysange who materialized the Collyn, of which, as of Gui also, you may hear more in *The High Place*.

THEN *The Way of Ecben* was finished in May 1929, and published in the October of the same year. For this story Garnier is of course my main source, although I borrowed a few of the more highly-colored details from Dr. Stewart's fine thesis upon the mythology of Rorn.

My decision to make an English prose version of *The Way of Ecben* sprang more or less directly, I think, from the discovery made in January 1929, when I came to preface *The Eagle's Shadow* for the Storisende edition of the Biography, that for some seventeen years I had avoided, quite unconsciously, the chivalrous attitude as a main theme.

"Let us return," I said, "to our first loves. I will paint me one more chevalier completely. Yes, and in dealing with the lovers of Ettarre, I will summarize, just as an overture rehearses those melodies which are to be developed later, the Biography's three leading themes."

I said then: "*The Music from Behind the Moon* is about Ettarre and the poet Madoc,—who may or who may not have been called Horvendile after the losing of his wealth, his wife, and his wits also. About that I do not know; I have not ever known much about Horvendile: but I do know that *The White Robe* deals with Ettarre and a Bishop of Valnères who was notably gallant. In logic therefore, now that I reach the eve of my fiftieth birthday, and bleak time permits me to complete but one more high-hearted story about Ettarre, I will put into English *The Way of Ecben*, which treats of Ettarre and of an Alfgar who was, above all, chivalrous."

And I said also: "Yes, it is fitting, inasmuch as the publishing of the Biography began in 1904 with a tale about Felix Kennaston and Margaret Hugonin, that I should now publish in 1929, as the last bit of the Biography which I shall ever publish, that strange tale, which Felix Kennaston put into verse, and which Margaret Hugonin caused to be printed, of *The King's Quest*."

Moreover, this saga had the advantage of suggesting in itself, I thought, some of the many reasons for my decision that after I had reached fifty there should be no more books about Poictesme or Lichfield, or about any more of the inheritors of Dom Manuel's life. The touch of time, about the effects of which you may read in *The Way of Ecben*, with a king as protagonist, does not spare writers either. The uncharitable may even assert that *The Way of Ecben* quite proves this fact: and indeed it is a privilege of which they have taken full benefit. In any case, now that the units of the long Biography of Dom Manuel's life added up to a neat twenty, which was convenient to the laws of Poictesme, and now that with a yet more coercive arithmetic the years of my own living added up to fifty, *The Way of Ecben* appeared to me the story most fit to commemorate the winding up of my twenty-eight years' sport with the Biography of the Life of Manuel.

So I did write *The Way of Ecben*: and we published it, with rare business acumen, in October 1929, upon the very day before the stock market crashed, and that which we term bewilderedly "the depression" set in, and book buying ceased for some while to be an American avocation.

NOW as a trilogy *The Witch-Woman* occupies in the Biography its set place with fair competence. Nevertheless, it is not the book as I first shaped it. I had meant *The Witch-Woman* to be a series of ten stories, which I had worked out more or less thoroughly; and which stories (now that *Something About Eve*, after being for ten years in composition, had at last gone to the printers, early in 1927) I intended to write at leisure, in time for the complete *Witch-Woman* to be published as a book in the spring of 1930. That gave me nearly three years in which to dispose of *The Witch-Woman*, a period which would suffice amply. But I had reckoned without taking into any due account the fond toil which I, like the tricked Norns, would have to give over to rewriting my own rather long book, in the form of the entire Biography, between the beginning of 1927 and the initial two months of 1930, for the Storisende edition.

It was not planned when we undertook this edition that I should do anything except supply a special preface and a signature for each volume: and a contribution thus limited would have satisfied everyone

concerned except only me. When I once began upon
this definitive version of the Biography I found that
I could not rest content with merely decorative
touches. I preferred to rewrite each book, whether
it were for the first or the second or the third occasion, entirely. Some of the volumes seemed to require
fewer alterations than did others, of course; upon
the whole I most thoroughly changed those of which
I was now producing my fourth printed version: but
every one of them did my untiring, and from any
practical standpoint my quite profitless, desire for
that continuous perfection such as no writer can ever
attain, compel me to rewrite throughout during
those very busy three years. This time-wasting, while
profoundly enjoyable, left me enough leisure in
which to complete in the shape of any new work only
The White Robe and *The Way of Ecben* before I
came to be fifty.

Upon that uncheery date I had very long ago
determined to end the Biography, for reasons which
you may find listed in the note on *Townsend of Lichfield*. In this way, because of my foible for rewriting
prose passages which as they stood would not seriously have outraged the standards of what many
persons unsmilingly term American literature, did
The Witch-Woman become a trilogy; and it remains
the sole known exception to the fixed law of Poictesme, that all things shall go by tens forever.

Well, but it follows that some three-fourths of

The Witch-Woman must remain always in John Charteris' library, among the unwritten books. I may tell you without any undue boasting that when I last visited Fairhaven the complete *Witch-Woman* stood in most excellent company, between John Milton's *King Arthur of Britain* and Frances Newman's *History of Sophistication*: and upon this rather rueful occasion a brief peep into the pages of *The Witch-Woman* convinced me that in the not ever electro-typed parts of this dizain were included, beyond any question, the very finest examples of my fiction-making.

The intended *Witch-Woman*, I observed, was a quite bulky volume. It was all written flawlessly, in prose which displayed a continuous perfection; and in brief, the complete *Witch-Woman* so favorably impressed me that I was at pains to copy out and to preserve at least this unique book's Table of Contents.

One admired, to begin with, a preface headed "Hail and Farewell, Ettarre!" in hardly anything resembling another expository paper which I have seen elsewhere under the same title. And the ten, all rather lengthy episodes which the book furthermore contained I found to be, in their proper order:— The Music from Behind the Moon; The Thirty-first of February; The Furry Thing That Sang; The Lean Hands of Volmar; The Holy Man Who Washed; The Little Miracle of St. Lesbia; The

White Robe; The Evasions of Ron; The Child Out
of Fire; and The Way of Ecben.

This much only I noted. Then I regretfully put
back the complete *Witch-Woman* in its right place,
between *King Arthur of Britain* (a truly sublime
drama which I have not ever read) and that *History
of Sophistication* which was dedicated to, of all persons, naïve me.

THIS never finished *Witch-Woman* was to have followed through several centuries the adventuring of
Ettarre and of Horvendile; and it would have told
how the immortal pair made sport with ten human
lovers of Ettarre who, howsoever differing in other
respects, yet one and all committed the grave error of
touching, and of striving to possess amorously, the
flesh-and-blood body which at that time Ettarre was
wearing. Well, and in the final outcome, this intended dizain has dwindled into a mere trilogy. I
regret the outcome.

Yes, I regret in all sincerity that from my typewriter will come no more stories about Ettarre, who
has been for so many years the most dear to me of
Dom Manuel's daughters. My comfort is that there
will always be new stories about Ettarre, under one
or another name, by the writers to get glory after
my decaying generation has entered finally its de-
creed limbo. All the young men everywhere that

were poets have had their glimpse of the witch-
woman's loveliness; they have heard a cadence or
two of that troubling music which accompanies the
passing of Ettarre; and they have made, and they
will make forever, their brave and passionate stories
about the witch-woman, so long as youth endures
among mankind and April returns punctually into
the fine world which young people inhabit.

But we who are not young any longer, and who
must behold Ettarre and all things else with the
eyes which time has given us, and who (despite how
many glowing memories) must yet find in her music,
nowadays, no more than did old Alfgar at his quest-
ing's end,—we may not dare to depend upon mere
memories, howsoever splendid and dear they may be
to us, for the piecing out of any more tales about
Ettarre the witch-woman. Our memories alone remain. We may well dare, as Alfgar dared, to preserve our faith in that which is beyond and above us:
but we would wiseliest keep faith, even so, in silence
as to that which our lean human senses deny nowadays. Our memories alone remain. We that have
come to middle life may not any longer behold Ettarre with that clearness which is granted to our
juniors: and this is an unpleasant fact, this is indeed
in some sort a taunt, which must, to-day and for all
time, obscurely discontent the living of every poet
who has entered into his prosaic and over-quiet fif-
ties, and who has discovered, quietly, that of the lad

who followed after Ettarre memories alone remain
nowadays.

Even so, it has been recorded what all these
maimed and discontented poets yet cry to the witch-
woman:

"We would have nothing changed. That loveliness
which we saw once and then lost forever, and that
music which we heard just once and might not ever
hear again, were things more fine than is contentment. Hail and farewell, Ettarre!"

Domnei

THIS volume deals primarily with the oldest of the three daughters of Dom Manuel, as her history is set forth in one of the romances ascribed to Nicolas de Caen. It is also the first of the volumes in the Biography which treat in particular of the inheritors of Manuel's life who assumed toward that inheritance what has been earlier described as the chivalrous attitude.

Of the birth and childhood of Dame Melicent the Biography has already recorded somewhat; and in *Domnei* you have a partial history of her womanhood. For it has appeared simpler—in the behalf of plain exposition—to approach the main theme of chivalry through sundry dealings, first, with that form of woman-worship called "domnei" which was a product of chivalry; and of which Melicent became in some sort the victim. This form of woman-worship is described in the book's Afterword with a particularity which does not demand repetition here.

Moreover, I have waived all disputing as to whether the tales in *The Silver Stallion* may right-

fully be attributed to Nicolas de Caen,—since for my
purpose this question does not matter one way or the
other. To the unprejudiced, however, it should be
fairly apparent, I think, that the author of *The Silver Stallion* could not possibly have been the same
person who wrote *Domnei*. There I am well content
to leave this matter, as being, in any final analysis,
an unarguable affair of taste and feeling rather than
of strict logic. We find, at all events, in *Domnei* no
least survival of faith in Dom Manuel as a spiritual
Redeemer. For Nicolas is supposed to have written
the chronicle upon which *Domnei* is based, I must
ask you to remember, in the latter part of the fif-
teenth century, a good hundred years after that cult
had gone the way of most religious faiths.

In the comprehensive pages of Verville—who, it
is perhaps unnecessary to state, believes, as I do not
believe, that Nicolas wrote the stories contained in
The Silver Stallion,—you may read of the ending of
Dom Manuel's career as a messiah; and of how the
cult of Manuel perished, as it were, overnight when,
in 1347, Dom Manuel's reputed great-grandson,
King Edward the Third of England, came into Southern France (at the head of an invading army of Eng-
lishmen) and the promises given to faith appeared
to have been kept fully by irony. For here was the
long hoped for reincarnation of Poictesme's large-
thewed Redeemer. Here was again the tall gray
hero, with the squinting left eye; and he had, as was

prophesied, a cortège of very terrible followers. Here in all material respects was just such a person as had been looked for: only, he came not to confer any celestial favoritism upon Poictesme, or any good upon any part of France, but rudely to pillage and destroy. Here was Manuel the Redeemer, to every appearance, returned into Poictesme: he returned, though, to burn Aradol and Naimes and to hang the ten syndics of Évre.

It was true that the King spared Aigremont, out of respect for the church and monastery of St. Hoprig; and that after his departure northward, when his lieutenants had failed to take Bellegarde after a six weeks' siege, Poictesme was not molested further. But, materially, quite enough hurt had been done to make the spiritual damage irreparable. Faith could not survive before a coincidence so vexatiously awkward: and Poictesme desired no more such returnings of the Redeemer.

Thus the cult of Manuel, as the land's future messiah, perished instantly: and by the time of Nicolas de Caen this cult, except as a matter of antiquarian interest, was remembered hardly anywhere in France.

Domnei was begun as early as 1910, but it was soon laid aside, so that I might collect in England, and put together in Virginia, the contents of a book concerned with another family than Dom Manuel's. *Domnei* was then finished in 1912,—if, indeed, a narrative so remarkably inconclusive may be said at any time to have been finished.

And the problem, "What happened afterward?" used to confront me ever and again for some years. When in 1919 I wrote The Wedding Jest (as that story now figures in *The Line of Love*) I surmised the answer, at least from Melicent's point of view. Yet I do not doubt that Perion regarded the entire matter from an angle noticeably different, inasmuch as some such discrepancy is the normal outcome of most love-matches.

Domnei, I repeat, was finished in 1912, among the coal mines of West Virginia, at the same time that *The Rivet in Grandfather's Neck* was being aspiringly touched up to meet with its natural defeat in the Reilly & Britton $10,000 prize contest for the best novel submitted to the firm during 1912: and of the two stories thus coincidently written, it was *Domnei* which went seeking a publisher for the fewer number of years. *Domnei,* if I may say this without appearing to boast, was rejected by no more than twelve publishers. They were all quite civil about it, too, although J. F. P., for Harper & Brothers, did write me, on 9 April 1912, with entire truth, yet, as I thought, a bit tactlessly,—"We have not found a sale for your books published by us heretofore which would encourage us to accept any new venture." To that, you see, there was a depressingly final ring . . . But I decline to establish the excellent business judgment of the eleven other firms by recording their names here, since in any case I have to record that the publisher who did eventually bring out this romance, in the autumn of 1913, under the title of *The Soul of Melicent*, sold precisely 493 copies.

I then did not quite understand this. I had already published two not over successful books and three books which had proved to be commercial calamities; and for that matter, I was destined to publish under the Norns' frowning yet five more volumes from which my sole increment would be a handful of patronizing or acrimonious press clippings. But never during the eighteen years which I devoted to failing at authorship, until prurience gave me a leg up from out of oblivion, was any one of my other books quite so whole-heartedly repudiated by the reading public as was *The Soul of Melicent*. And it seemed to me at this period, I confess, that through some concerted and really earnest effort, the publishers might have sold the usual 500 copies.

But the fall season of 1913, I find, upon consultation of the back files of the *Publisher's Weekly*, to have been opulent in fiction of the first importance. *Pollyanna,* the Glad Book, for example, was then at the height of its artistic success; and with the not wholly unselfish aid of the L. C. Page Publishing Company, "Mr. John Wanamaker, the Eminent Merchant and Honorary President of the Pollyanna Glad Club" was exhorting the book-buying public at large, in a sensible business-like fashion, "Just read *Pollyanna*; and you will be able to make your home and store—your whole life—feel the thrill of it." Selling almost abreast of *Pollyanna* in the latter part of 1913 was *Their Yesterdays*, in which the vigor and kindliness and power and grace of Dr. Harold Bell Wright's preceding masterworks were admitted —by his publishers, Messrs. Reilly & Britton—to be woven into a strain more delicate and more beautiful than this great writer had ever before penned; and through which Dr. Wright told more plainly than ever before the secrets and joys of his big heart.

Yes, and not only Dr. Wright was about the weaving of masterpieces in 1913. In that same fall season, I find, the Century Company was conceding that Mrs. Frances Hodgson Burnett's happy fancy had never before woven so delightful and appealing a tale; nor had her magic pen ever written with such skill and charm, as in *T. Tembaron*, then to be found upon every well-appointed drawing-room table. Yet again had the greatest novel by the greatest American novelist just been published—upon this occasion by Appleton's, in the form of *The Business of Life* by Mr. Robert W. Chambers. Putnam's were bringing out *The Broken Halo*, and displaying a justifiable

pride, along with a portrait of the author, in this love
story so full of those fine qualities of the soul, and
the sustained idealism, and the transforming beauty
of thought, which had made Mrs. Florence L. Bar-
clay's characters the most lovable in fiction for many
hundreds of thousands of readers. There is really
some excellent reading in the back files of the *Publisher's Weekly*.

Besides that, the far-flung printing presses of civilization were groaning, in eleven European languages
and in Japanese, under *The Woman Thou Gavest
Me*, which Lippincott's granted to be "a really Great
Novel, for all the world and for all time," inasmuch
as this High-Water Mark of Hall Caine's Stupendous Genius presented The Most Superb Analysis of Modern Marriage Ever Written, and revealed
The Entire Relation of Man to Woman from the
Cradle to the Grave. And Doubleday, Page & Company (I find also, as I pursue my archæological
studies) were producing, with an advance sale prior
to publication of 163,000 copies, *Laddie*, a True
Blue Story, by Mrs. Gene Stratton Porter, very close
to the heart of nature, in flower and bird, and to the
heart of man in the purest and best emotions of life,
with four illustrations in color . . . So it followed
naturally enough that, in the excitement attendant
upon the delivery to the world of so many important
books, the reading public could not rationally waste
time on minor fiction. *The Soul of Melicent* perhaps

did quite as well as could be expected when, under, as it were, the hoofs of plenary and unconquerable competition, it reached a sale of 493 copies.

Meanwhile *The Soul of Melicent* was of course "remaindered": and for some six years thereafter I was continually encountering in bookshops this *Soul of Melicent* penciled at one or another candidly disparaging evaluation. It never, though, to my best knowledge, sold at less than nineteen cents; and book collectors tell me that the volume's fair market value has since risen beyond this sum, if the book be in good condition and have the dark blue binding of the "first state."

IN ANY case, the story was reissued, in 1920, in the Kalki edition, and its original manuscript title was then restored. To me this romance stayed always *Domnei*: but its first publishers had objected, quite reasonably, that *Domnei* was a title which no prospective book buyer could well get straight. They therefore—not quite so reasonably, as affairs turned out—had preferred to publish it as *The Soul of Melicent*. Not quite so reasonably, I submit, because this title too nobody ever did get straight. Through some odd form of metempsychosis it became *The Soul of Millicent*, where alone it was ever mentioned, in the "marked down" and the "special bargain" lists of all rash book dealers who had ordered a copy of this romance.

Well, and I indulged then in the profitless pleasure of saying, "I told you so." Yet, inasmuch as since the restoration of the book's first title it is customarily listed as *Dominie*, I fear that no really clear-cut moral is available.

Chivalry

AS ITS title indicates, this volume of the Biography continues to deal with the chivalrous attitude toward human existence. It takes up, after some additional traffic with that Alianora of Provence whom Manuel more or less loved, the line of those English monarchs who, as rumor said, were the inheritors of Dom Manuel's life on the wrong side of the blanket; and its concern is, in particular, with the women committed to the forlorn experiment of matrimony with these Manuelites—as that fine, foiled genius, John Macy, elected to christen the tribe of Manuel.

Yet, since this volume has already a formal preface, under the heading Precautional, here seems to be very small need for me to describe the intended scope of *Chivalry*. It is, in brief, a book about people who believed themselves to be the children of God put under an obligation, during their temporary visit to Earth, to live as became members of His family. They did not always keep this obligation; yet at no time did they question its existence. So did

it color all their living, in ways which human beings
can still partly imagine and still partly observe, nowadays, but not actually comprehend any longer.

OF THESE tales The Story of the Fox-Brush was the
earliest written, in November 1904. The Story of
the Sestina was completed during the following December: whereafter *Chivalry* was put aside, in favor
of an intended full-length romance dealing with that
Queen who immediately preceded Alianora on the
throne of England. Toward the end of 1905, however, the manuscript of this not ever completed
comedy concerning Isabella of Angoulême and her
two husbands, John Lackland and Hugh de Lusignan,
was burned by its unapproving author; and the young
man who then wore my name returned to *Chivalry*.
The Story of the Housewife was next written, in the
January of 1906, although I find the note from
which this story was eventually developed to have
been thus recorded very early in 1904:

"Remember to write the story of John Copeland,
out of Froissart; making the whole affair turn on a
jesting offer of Edward III to give him, in exchange
for the King of Scots, a certain woman's hand in
marriage. Philippa would have a personal interest
in representing David as her captive,—to shake the
Countess of Salisbury's influence?"

Philippa, I can but deduce, was unaccountably pro-

moted from playing a blackguardly part in this story
to become its heroine. How that happened, I do not
at all remember.

After this note, by the bye, with about equally
staggering incoherence, follows straightway the title
and some suggestions as to the general atmosphere
of *Gallantry*,—which book might advantageously
combine, I observe it is stated in my own handwrit-
ing, all the better features of Congreve and Alfred
de Musset and Molière. That is a sentiment with
which I agree: yet in youth one really does cherish
a fair conceit of one's own ability, I reflect as I read
this naïve memorandum. The young author, in that
far-off spring of 1904, then immediately continued
in friendly exhortation to himself to remember to
write,

"Also, a mediæval dizain modeled roughly on
Massucio [*sic*] in his Novellino,—try a comic story
and a supernatural one. (Roger of Wendover ought
to furnish a suggestion for the latter.) Whole affair
purporting to be from the Contes of an imaginary
Frenchman (Englishman?) of the early sixteenth
century; and called *Chivalry*."

—All which extracts go to prove that a romanticist does not always follow out his original intentions to a hair's breadth. The remainder of
Chivalry, in any case, was written in 1906-7—in the
same unordered fashion, taking up whichsoever
seemed handiest of the now completely planned

series,—until the lateliest done of these tales, The
Story of the Scabbard, was finished early in the spring
of 1907.

THESE stories appeared in *Harper's Monthly Magazine*, at irregular intervals, between August 1905 and
April 1909, the more thanks to the then lately perfected method of reproducing paintings "in full
color." They were stories which the world-famous
illustrator, Howard Pyle, at that time under an
annual contract with Harper & Brothers, could
adorn sumptuously with his brightly tinted pictures.
So as reading matter these stories fairly well suited
the needs of *Harper's Monthly Magazine* at this
period, because Howard Pyle could make for them
such pictures, in exceedingly "full color," as at this
period were so widely marvelled over by all magazine readers that nobody had any special need to
bother about the faults or the defects of the accompanying text,—except, to be sure, the hapless illustrator, upon whom was foisted the necessity of more
or less reading this text before he had palliated it
with his paintings.

Well, and it was this same necessity which by-and-
by proved fatal to my quasi-connection with *Harper's
Monthly Magazine*. I touch here upon a matter
necessarily so lethal to any author's self-esteem that
my admiration for candor proves hardly a sufficing

spur to urge the approach. Yet the unconcealable fact remains that Howard Pyle, after some five years of continually illustrating my stories, felt that he could not afford to go on wasting the maturity of his genius upon such impermanent writings. He had put up with the ungrateful labor of making pictures which the more imaginative might regard as illustrating *The Line of Love*; and yet again the flare of his color-work had fitfully illuminated the unexplored depths of *Gallantry*. But *Chivalry*, it must here be confessed, proved, in that striking phrase familiar to all really well educated persons, the last straw.

So, after finishing the two illustrations which were to accompany The Story of the Scabbard, Howard Pyle sought relief from our joint paymasters, and explained to them, in the April of 1907:

"I am now at the height of my powers . . . I do not think it right for me to spend so great a part of my time in manufacturing drawings for magazine stories which I cannot regard as having any really solid or permanent value. Mr. Cabell's stories . . . are neither exactly true to history nor exactly fanciful, and while I have made the best illustrations for them which I am capable of making, I feel that they are not true to mediæval life, and that they lack a really permanent value such as I should now endeavor to present to the world."

His scruples were honored. Howard Pyle was soothed by being commissioned to illustrate a higher

class of fiction, that had really permanent value, in
the short stories of Marjorie Bowen and of Basil
King and of Bryan Hooker and of Thomas V. Briggs
and in Howard Pyle's own short stories; and H. M.
Alden, at that time the editor of *Harper's Monthly
Magazine*, began to find, seriatim and with all
civility, the tales now included in *The Certain Hour*
to be not sufficiently up to my earlier standards, even
as exhibited in these *Chivalry* stories, to make *The
Certain Hour* stories "available."

I record all this frankly and in, as it were, the
teeth of my self-esteem, because I am conscious
to-day that I owe a great deal to Howard Pyle. Of
the thirteen stories by me which he illustrated he
made excellent pictures for two or three; and besides
that, he was invariably gracious in communicating to
me the delight with which he had illustrated each
successive story. Yet neither of these facts is the true
cause of my gratitude.

I am grateful upon grounds rather more serious.
After some six years of contributing a short story
every month or so to the august and everywhere
well-thought-of pages of *Harper's Monthly Magazine*, I was unavoidably in train to become an "established" magazine writer, when this preservatory
protest by Howard Pyle, against illustrating any
more of my fiction, caused me—metaphorically, of
course—to be bundled neck and crop down the long
spiral stairs of the old Harper & Brothers' offices in

Franklin Square. And I really can discover, after looking over the roster of the American Institute of Arts and Letters, no "established" magazine contributor of that era who came to any honorable æsthetic ending.

THE quiet but never-sleeping terror of human nature and of human anatomy, and indeed of almost all biological facts, was far too great for any writer to resist; and it labored, with a quiet stubbornness, to restrict every character in magazine fiction to possessing, corporeally, just hands, feet, and a face. It follows that I look back, nowadays, with flat disbelief at the kind of editing then in vogue.

I recall how the first story which I submitted to *Harper's Monthly Magazine* was found acceptable except for the solecism of accrediting Sir John Falstaff with a belly. I do not mean that the authority of Shakespeare upon this point was disputed, or that any explicit slenderness was demanded as a matter of good form: it was merely that in the pages of a magazine "with a circulation so general as ours" the utmost which could decently be, and ultimately was, allowed even to Falstaff in the year of grace 1902 was a paunch.

I recall how the second piece of fiction which I submitted to the same periodical—that episode which in *The Line of Love* is called Adhelmar at Puysange

—was rejected because, in its first version, this story's deplorable heroine, Mélite de Puysange, was already married to Hugues d'Arques. That was a circumstance, I can assure you, which in the accompanying letter of rejection flowered handsomely into paternal rebuke. Yet do you not misunderstand me. I was not accredited with incurable turpitude. My return to the fold was still hoped for. It was simply that, in allowing a married woman to kiss, not merely once but upon three separate occasions, a man who was not her husband, I had indulged, it was gently conveyed to me—even at that early date—in carnal fancies which, from every reputable editorial standpoint in 1902, were obscene and lewd and lascivious and indecent.

It was admitted that such erudite persons as Henry Mills Alden and myself knew that, in the period and scene of the story, a kiss amounted to rather less if anything than a handshake: but that was not the point. The point which disposed of this and of every other question of fourteenth century etiquette was the point that *Harper's Monthly Magazine* was "read by all members of the family." So I was advised to, and I eventually did, preserve the moral tone appropriate for "a magazine with a circulation so general as ours" by somewhat postponing the wedding of Mélite, and by thus making her betrothed but not as yet married at the time of her three osculations. In this way was her conduct elevated into blameworthy light-mindedness, from its earlier levels of sheer depravity.

I recall how the "availability" of story after story was found to pivot upon one or another just such niggling and fantastic requirement, always in order to avoid shocking the morbid moral sensibility which, it was editorially assumed, with a quiet frank lifting of editorial shoulders, raged pandemically among the subscribers to *Harper's Monthly Magazine*. And I recall, too, that after a while I began now and then to submit a story which in no special passage was found to be unsuited for reading aloud when a family of subscribers had gathered cosily under the gas-jets, before the Latrobe stove. I was learning, without knowing it, just what regrettable veracities as to man's needs as a mammal had to be gingerly skirted, or ignored, or lied about, in the liveries of "a magazine with a circulation so general as ours." And I suspect that, in an additional year or two, I would have been honoring all these insane taboos, as mere axioms of good taste and refinement, with entire self-approval.

But, as it happened, in the very last nick of occasion, Howard Pyle requested that for the future the height of his powers and his paintings of really permanent value should no longer be wasted on my trivialities. He thus deprived me overnight of my six-year-old market; but he decisively preserved me

from becoming an esteemed contributor to the best-
thought-of magazines in the era of the greater
Roosevelt.

MEANWHILE, of the nine stories contained in *Chivalry*, six needed, before their primal appearance in
electrotype, some rather careful rewriting under editorial supervision, inasmuch as all six dealt with an
intimacy between a married woman and a male person
whom no ecclesiastic had licensed to enter her bed-
room. The Story of the Scabbard, wherein Gwyllem's
intentions were unmistakably extra-legal, had to be
made presentable, not by any feather-brained author,
but by the judicious pen of H. M. Alden himself,
before a theme so unsavory could be touched upon
in the pages of "a magazine with a circulation so
general as ours." That phrase, I can assure you, had
come by this time to represent to me a supreme and
all-embracing, if incomprehensible, law; that phrase
included, in fact, a complete code of laws which I
revered humbly without knowing just what they were.
And The Story of the Choices required a particularly thorough disinfecting, because in the story's
first form Queen Ysabeau was unfaithful to her marriage vows with a candor inadmissible into any fiction which was not printed either as history or as the
main news of the day in the morning paper.

THESE stories, then, were collected in volume form; and they were first published, in the autumn of 1909, as an illustrated "Christmas Book," when this collection of mediæval romances—for reasons not ever clear to me—was vended in a red cardboard box upon the lid of which, in yet another painting by Howard Pyle, a cavalier of the English Restoration period was attempting (with the depravity only too characteristic of that licentious era) to hold the hand of a contemporaneously clothed young woman. Several dozen copies of *Chivalry* were sold. Nor do I think that very many hundreds of copies were "remaindered," because the first, and only, Harper edition was small.

In 1922 *Chivalry* was reissued by McBride's, in the unillustrated Kalki edition; and I then took occasion to recast these tales. Still later it was permitted me to rewrite this book yet again, for the Storisende edition, without being bothered by any special taboos of any kind; so that nowadays you may read these stories (with their diction a thought bettered) very much as they were first imagined by me when they were not publishable in America. I venture to hope that, in to-day's rather less squeamish atmosphere, their enormities will mount no crimson banners in the cheek of innocence and will sound reasonably few alarums to the pulses of the constitutionally lascivious.

And I venture, too, to point out that these stories,

no less than *Beyond Life*, are written "in character."
In one and all the stories which are attributed to
this Nicolas de Caen, was made the attempt to honor
faithfully, alike in the method of narration and in
the point of view, the quaint notions of Nicolas de
Caen rather than what I take to be the equally quaint
notions of his American transcriber.

Jurgen

UPON reflection I have decided denyingly as to the world's possible need of any further comment by me upon *Jurgen*. Otherwise, I would here explain that the writer whom I have seen identified, in some place or another, as "the author of *Jurgen*" aimed with this volume to develop at full length in the Biography a leaven of gallantry, as well as yet further to foreshadow every poet's fundamental attitude toward life. For *Jurgen* deals with Dom Manuel's second daughter, Dorothy la Désirée, whose forte it was to inspire—and, for that matter, to participate in—gallantry.

And I would explain, too, that to each of the daughters of Manuel is allotted in the Biography her province. As Ettarre la Beale remains, forever, the dream of all true poets, so did Dame Melicent in her day prompt her adorers to chivalry; and so did Dorothy la Désirée incite, not only many lighter gallantries, but also, as Jurgen has phrased it in *The Silver Stallion*, "a variation upon the Grail legend . . . and a hungering and a dreaming that will not die, and a laughter which derides its utterer." In the book *Jurgen* you have the gist of this epic: and I believe the considerate will note this Dorothy la Désirée, howsoever infrequent her corporeal entrances, to remain throughout this narrative its most important character . . . Nay, more: I would have pointed out—in the commentary which I do not elect to write—that this Dorothy is very actually, in the phrase which I do not love, "the author of *Jurgen*." For light women have their invaluable uses, the more especially in the forming of poets, who one and all derive, even nowadays, their aberrations from Troy Town. Thus, it is of Helen that they dream, of that sweet tacit queen, tall, brightly colored and impalpable, and as forever ageless as any other mist tatter: but it was a Cressida who shaped them, and who made each poet vocal, as well as, at the last pinch, ruthless. To this rule there is no possible exception: and all fine literature—together, to be sure, with most of its lower branches—was mothered by one or another wanton.

I am tempted here to digress, into cataloguing those beneficent ladies whose prettiness and whose fond unfaith, ever since the heyday of Catullus, have materially enriched our libraries; and thus, through a pleasing fog of remarkably elegant language, to escape from my proper task of contriving for *Jurgen* some brand-new commentary. I am indissuadably set against ever writing any more about *Jurgen*.

OTHERWISE—in that not yet written commentary—
I would be recording hereabouts that *Jurgen* was begun in the March of 1918, and completed in the
October of the same year. The manuscript stayed
in my desk drawer, though, for some time thereafter,
so as to allow for the publication of *Beyond Life*;
and it in consequence received a liberal amount of
retouching during the first part of 1919. Meanwhile
a portion of the first chapter and of the chapters
recording Jurgen's third entrance into the cave were
shaped into the semblance of a short story, and the
result was published, in the July 1918 issue of the
old *Smart Set*, under the auspices of H. L. Mencken,
who thus assumed the responsibility for Jurgen's
début in print.

The book was brought out in September 1919,
and rather promptly got into trouble . . . All this,
though, is recorded in *Jurgen and the Law*; so that
here is no need for me to rehearse Jurgen's not unremarkable career in the Court of General Sessions
of the Peace in and for the County of New York.

MOREOVER—I repeat—I am indissuadably set against
writing any more about this *Jurgen*, to which "the
author of *Jurgen*" has become in some degree a
satellite. It is, the majority assure me, immeasurably
the best of all this author's books, so much so, in-

deed, that the other books are in comparison not particularly worth reading . . . Thereafter I in meditation may permissibly go so far, now and then, as to echo the verdict of the young Duke of Logreus concerning the people of Glathion: but I emulate, too, his wise taciturnity. I bow to the immutable law that the true worth of any book, even of such sad stuff as seems to me to compose *Don Quixote* and *Pride and Prejudice* and *Tom Jones*, and a number of yet other world-famous literary masterpieces, depends not upon what the author has put into its pages but upon what one or another reader, for one or another reason, gets out of them. And I do not press the point that this *Jurgen* seems to me not truly an individual book but just a chapter in the Biography of the Life of Manuel.

Meanwhile, however, with that slight but necessary aloofness characteristic of every satellite, "the author of *Jurgen*" is condemned to refrain from any criticism of *Jurgen*; and so lacks, I take it, all matter for any possible commentary. The opinions of a Frankenstein upon the topic of monsters are open to suspicion. And meanwhile, too, I look with lively and with rather wistful interest upon the very first draft of the book which actually did give its writer, after eighteen years, more or less of a literary career, and which ultimately became this yet-uncommented-upon *Jurgen*.

THE thing covers, in all, just two sheets of "examination pad" paper: and viewing these half-forgotten 'pencilings, it seems droll enough to consider this half-ounce of wood-pulp which epitomizes—according to your point of view—the fœtus of my ill-fame or else the sole arguable excuse for my existence. In either aspect the thing seems a bit inadequate.

Across the top of the first page I find written: "Go to the Devil"—"Some Ladies and Jurgen"—"The Pawnbroker's Shirt." And I recall, now, that each of these titles—along with "A Year from Wednesday" —was a title which at one or another time the author of *Jurgen* once tentatively accorded to this volume.

Then I discover that the book was originally planned in ten long chapters with an epilogue; for after the possible titles these divisions are painstakingly listed. I record them just as they stand, employing italics to show the canceled words:

"How Jurgen Was Rid of the Plague of His Life.

"How Jurgen Returned to (*?the Kingdom*) the Garden between Dawn and Sunrise (*?Nessus*).

"How Jurgen Won a Gift from Mother Sereda (*?Visited Mother Wednesday*).

"How Jurgen Rescued a (*Won to the Far*) Princess (from the buried galley) (Guenevere) (his foreknowledge).

"How Jurgen Served (*the*) a Sorceress (Anaïtis) (= Morgaine la Fée) (*?Nimuë*).

"How Jurgen Loved (*the*) a Dryad (& saw Queen Helen in Leukê).

"How Jurgen (*Sank*) Was Cast into (*Hell*) the Hell of his Fathers (succuba).

"How Jurgen (*Rose to Heaven*) Got into his Grandmother's Heaven (?Paradise).

"How Jurgen Took Counsel with His Shadow (Sereda).

"How Jurgen Found Koshchei:—(Guenevere, Anaïtis & Helen).

"How Jurgen Sat by the Fire."

And I find also that parts three to nine are enclosed in a large bracket beside which is written, "Youth & the double shadow." It thus seems that Jurgen, once, in his false youth was accompanied by two shadows. What they were like, or how he acquired them, I have forgotten.

THEN, evidently, with his outline fairly established, the yet youngish person who wrote *Jurgen* in 1918 must have set down the various "points" of the intended book just as they occurred to him, for the next paragraph begins abruptly:

"The Sorceress shows him Helen—?hourglass—the devils in their shapes and traits—Jacob's Ladder —day in the forest—his dead loves—Raknar, crowned, & at his feet three chests of silver—Ex-

calibur—the talisman & Lisa—chair & chess board
—Cocaigne is the summer home of Anaïtis."

So do I discover that the Thragnar of the book
was originally Raknar, come out of the *Barda Saga*
with his loot from the *Saga of Hromund Greipson*.
I remember that "the Sorceress" passed through a
brief season of being Cleopatra, on her way to becoming Anaïtis . . . But that "day in the forest"
puzzles me. Then, very cloudily, I recollect that, still
in a version of the book which was never put down
upon paper, Gogyrvan Gawr accorded to the rescuer
of his daughter a day quite alone with her in the
Druid forest, upon the understanding that no questions were to be asked afterward as to their sylvan
recreations. I recall how at sunset Jurgen, with the
girl yet in his arms, heard from afar the horns of the
approaching cavalcade which came to fetch young
Guenevere to Arthur's court; and how Jurgen, as a
well-seasoned reader of romance, foreknew, in the
moment that she protested her undying love for him,
all which was to befall this Guenevere during the
remainder of her life. And I imagine that this notion
was transmogrified a little by a little, as the book
advanced, until in a variant form this notion had
been transferred to the present seventh chapter,
where the essentials of this notion remain, but concern quite another young woman.

In brief, only "the talisman" gravels me. I can
recollect nothing whatever about it. And, plainly, the

author's allusion cannot well be to Jurgen's cantrap, since with the cantrap Lisa is in no way connected.

The next three, very brief paragraphs, however, seem to have been adhered to faithfully enough. It is obvious that "the author of *Jurgen*" is here about his "time-plot," and is fitting the travels of his hero to the transitions of the sun.

"?Even year in all—Walburga's Eve—May Day —(Cameliard) May to 21 June—(Cocaigne) 21 June to 22 September—(Leukê) 22 September to 22 December—(Hell) 22 December to 22 March— & to Heaven (37 days) 30 April—May Day."

All this seems comprehensible enough. In practice, to be sure, it proved impossible to imagine how Jurgen would employ himself during thirty-seven whole days in Heaven, and that difficulty had to be got around . . . But "the author of *Jurgen*" had added, with conspicuous inconsequence:

"The Mass—the boat journey to Cocaigne—the beach & the wall.

"He repeats in epitome his real life, that is, in the face of memory, does all that he regrets, all over again."

THEREAFTER follows just one paragraph, but a tremendously long one:

"Jurgen comes upon Helen asleep—his grandmother for whom Heaven was made—the protestants against error, who cast the Greek gods into Hell—Sereda to Merlin is Dana—Pan in the forest —the two children of Anaïtis, with whom Jurgen amuses himself when she is preoccupied by her social duties, as involved in religious ceremonies—Jurgen as ghost of Gogyrvan's grandfather, who had 'known' Jurgen's grandmother—the riffraff about Anaïtis—The Breaking of the Veil—Sereda seen as Cybele, that is, the world—in the hourglass the sands turn to vapor & rise—Jurgen is made small & enters, so that he walks in a desert, then among boulders—?stripped of the non-essentials—leaves Excalibur (?or Caliburn) with Anaïtis—Varvara is sister to Melicent & Ettarre—Second chapter at Storisende, third at Bellegarde—Hell is made for those who believe in the importance of their own sins, & Jurgen talks with his father there—in Paradise are only his grandmother's ideas, he being among them—the devils & the angels confess to being illusions provided by Koshchei, who admires pride & love because these are emotions unattainable by him when he contemplates the universe for which he is responsible—the Furies are the daughters of Anaïtis, delightful little girls—in Leukê Helen is wedded to Achilles—at Storisende are Townsend & Stella, & Rudolph & Anne—he goes into the forest to learn All—for Anaïtis he fights the Master Philologist & is defeated—Jurgen talks with Varvara on the way home, & end with Jurgen peeping in the window at Lisa & the house set in order—he sighs & enters."

And that, word for word, completes the primal draft of *Jurgen*.

NOW, as I regard this last long paragraph, I note, first of all, that Dorothy la Désirée seems to have come originally, with Sereda, out of Russia, and to have been called Varvara; then, that Sereda too had once another name, having somehow adventured into Celtic mythology; that the family of Anaïtis increased with noticeable speed during the setting down of this paragraph; and that a new ending—still not quite the ending of the present book—was now being devised for the story, to replace that first-thought-of epilogue in which old Jurgen nodded peacefully beside his snug hearth-fire. I observe too that the notion of Jurgen's actually going into the hourglass of Time (instead of travelling with the Equinox), and of his being stripped of his non-essentials, and of his thus dwindling in size—with the grains of sand he trod upon becoming always relatively larger and larger, until at last a midget was toiling toward Helen among veritable boulders—that this notion seems to have many possibilities, of which, for one reason or another, "the author of *Jurgen*" did not avail himself. I am sure I do not know why.

Yet, upon the whole, *Jurgen* appears to have developed logically enough from that first draft, with far fewer futile blunderings into blind alleys as the tale developed than, as I have elsewhere recorded, are revealed by the notes made for *Figures of Earth*.

That, anyhow, is the entire first draft of *Jurgen*. So I transcribe it here unchanged. And I placatingly allow my original, quite harmless intentions, just as they were in 1918, to supply for *Jurgen* the place of that not-yet-written commentary which I am indissuadably set against ever writing. We have it upon excellent authority that everybody ought to be judged —after all—by his intentions.

The Line of Love

WITH this volume the Biography passes to the life of Dom Manuel as it was perpetuated through ten generations, and as this life exemplified, in turn, the gallant, the chivalrous and the poetic attitude. It is not necessary, I trust, for me here to distinguish, after all that John Charteris and I have said as to these three possible attitudes toward human existence. It seems plain enough that, as Florian and Falstaff and Raymond d'Arnaye and the tenth Marquis of Falmouth lived in that atmosphere of genial compromise which is the essence of gallantry, just so were Adhelmar and Fulke d'Arnaye and Will Sommers the adherents of chivalrous ideals: whereas it stays, even nowadays, a matter of rather general knowledge that Marlowe and Villon were poets.

Yet *The Line of Love*, alone among the many books which I have published—a heading under which it is forbidden me to include *The Witch-Woman*—presents all three of the attitudes almost equally, where the other volumes of the Biography specialize in one or another of this trinity. *The Line*

of Love may thus, in some sense, be regarded as the
Biography in miniature. And that, indeed, is natural
enough, since this, the earliest of my books in point
of composition, is the germ of the Biography, and the
seed from which all has grown, a little by a little, into
tolerable completeness.

I CONTEMPLATE the Biography as it now stands. In
Beyond Life I can see a preface which discusses in
logic pretty much every matter that the Biography
reveals in action; and which in particular concerns
the frail human logic behind the gallant, the chivalrous and the poetic solutions of human existence.
Then in *Figures of Earth* and *The Silver Stallion* is
comprised the entire career of Manuel, as he appeared in the eyes of those who knew him best in life,
and, also, as he appeared in the eyes of those same
persons, and of yet other persons, after his passing
out of life . . . Yet Manuel himself, I would have
you note, remains unexplained to the very last. I can
find, in these two volumes dealing with the uneffusive
and aloof Redeemer of Poictesme, merely what other
people saw and thought of this man who—living
among chivalrous conditions—appeared to some persons most brilliantly to exemplify the theory of divine
vicarship, and to yet other persons seemed to be the
creation of his fellows' stupidity. I take neither side;
and I stay content to leave Manuel, in common with

all Redeemers, more or less an enigma, not ever solved with completeness.

Turning thence toward the descendants of Manuel, the trilogy of *The Witch-Woman* presents, in epitome, the three strivings in which the descendants of Manuel are hereafter to be involved; but in particular does *The Witch-Woman* outline the poet's attitude toward life, as it is determined by Dom Manuel's third daughter. In *Domnei* and in *Chivalry* I find the perpetuated life of Manuel concerned, at more length and a deal more directly, with the two main tenets of the chivalrous attitude,—with woman-worship and with the notion of one's final responsibility to a divine Father.

Then Jurgen—he whose over-plastic nature was remodeled everywhere by the soft hands of Dom Manuel's second and least admirable daughter—attempts to live gallantly for a quite extensive number of book pages. Well, and it is an attempt in which he neither succeeds nor fails: for Jurgen gives over the game, of his own will, before the game has been played out; handing in as his own personal judgment upon the merits of gallantry the Scots verdict of "Not Proven." And here, in *The Line of Love*, the life of Manuel is concerned with all three attitudes throughout the course of (after the favored number of Poictesme) ten generations.

I glance toward the later volumes. *The High Place* and *Gallantry* return to yet clearer examples of the gallant attitude, and appraise it, severally, in its failure and in its relative success. Just so do *Something About Eve* and *The Certain Hour* then illustrate the failure, and, from at least the standpoint of an Economist, the success, of the poet's attitude toward life.

In *The Cords of Vanity* (with its appendices, *From the Hidden Way* and *The Jewel Merchants*) I find a portrait of the gallant person in modern conditions, precisely as *The Rivet in Grandfather's Neck* depicts enmired in very much the same conditions the chivalrous person. *The Jewel Merchants* stands a little apart, by virtue of its form; yet this play speaks with decision the last word as to gallantry, and as to what gallantry becomes when it is uninhibited; for the Duke is but Townsend freed from every nature of restraint.

Then, with *The Eagle's Shadow* and *The Cream of the Jest*, the story of the Biography is rounded off, just as the long story began, with yet another two-volume comedy, presenting the poet in modern conditions,—and presenting, also, the manner of this Felix Kennaston's return into Poictesme, whereby the life of Manuel ends its seven long centuries of journeying at the point of its outset. An epilogue follows, in the form of *Straws and Prayer-Books*, which explains—with something, it may be, of the uneasy volubility with which we all explain our mistakes—why the Biography was written.

Yes: to me the Biography appears a tolerably complete and symmetrical affair, an affair of three main themes regarded each from a quartet of varying standpoints. It would perhaps have been better, in a world wherein the obtuse have, after all, their claims to be humored, to have called the Biography *The Life of Manuel.* The delusion seems but too prevalent that a biography is necessarily an autobiography. Yet, in any case, it is droll to reflect how all developed from *The Line of Love.*

BY MY count, I repeat, *The Line of Love* is the earliest of my books. Of the seven stories which the original version contained, five were completed before *The Eagle's Shadow* was begun; and the other two were written while *The Eagle's Shadow* was yet in course of composition, so that the typescript of *The Line of Love* was in the hands of its publishers in April 1904, a good six months before the appearance of my first published book. It thus seems to me that the second of my books to appear in print was the earliest in point of composition . . . I mean, of course, in its original form. When I fall to weighing the claims of the present *Line of Love* with its two stories added in 1921, against the claims of the present *Eagle's Shadow*, with its Appendix (so humiliatingly more rich in humor than is anything else in the book) and its large proportion of new matter as added in 1923

—over. and above the fact that both books were yet again rewritten for the Storisende edition, in 1928-9 —why, then I face a problem before which my lean mathematics falter. There seems no solution possible: and I cannot estimate by what system of logic either book could be declared the earlier production.

—To which statement I append a hasty postscript: I do not think it at all matters.

THE first of these stories was Love-Letters of Falstaff, written in November 1901. This was one of the five tales which in that month I completed and mailed simultaneously to five different magazines, as the formal opening of my literary career. Three of them, by an astounding and in the end, I suspect, a disastrous coincidence, were accepted. The other two, after they had been rejected some thirty-odd times, by really intelligent editors, I destroyed.

Adhelmar at Puysange and The Conspiracy of Arnaye followed in, respectively, the January and the April of 1902. The Castle of Content and In Ursula's Garden were done in the September and October of that year. The series was then laid aside for *The Eagle's Shadow.* I returned to *The Line of Love* in December 1903, when In Necessity's Mortar was written. "Sweet Adelais" was then done in January 1904; and the book, in its first form, was forthwith completed.

Meanwhile each of the stories had been—finally —sold to *Harper's Monthly Magazine* under the general conditions which I have indicated in commenting upon *Chivalry*. The book itself was accepted by Harper & Brothers in the May of 1904 . . . For I appear in those days to have kept remarkably exact accounts. I thus find as concerns this volume the business-like entry: "Submitted to Harper and Brothers April 4, 1904; accepted by them May 14, 1904; to be delivered Oct. 1st. Magazine receipts on these stories, in all, $580.00." . . . Well, and the final revised "copy" was delivered punctually, I have no doubt, on "Oct. 1st" 1904: but *The Line of Love* was not published until almost a year later, appearing in September 1905.

It was held over, I remember, from the spring to the fall season of 1905 because that dreadful product of misguided ingenuity known as a "Christmas Book" was then widely popular. *The Line of Love* was therefore issued with the illustrations "in full color" which Howard Pyle had made for three of the stories when they first appeared in *Harper's Monthly Magazine*. An L-shaped segment was naïvely lopped from each picture so as to reduce it from magazine- to book-size. Each page of the book was strangled with a floral bordering of improbable vegetation indecisively tinted somewhere between red and yellow; the book's binding masterfully combined the largest possible assortment of color with the least possible restraint; and the completed, rather appalling product was marketed in a pasteboard box of tumultuous crimson.

It was, though, marketed. I must record that, for an expensive two-dollar book, at a time when the average new book sold for $1.07, *The Line of Love* met with a mild success. It so happened that Mark Twain thought well of the volume, and wrote a kindly word or two in praise of it: and a bit later that President named Roosevelt who was the pet of a nation's fondness, not the punishment of its folly, the great genial Theodore himself, commended to his people *The Line of Love.* Under a sponsorship so august, the book actually "sold" throughout the fall season of 1905, to the extent of some 2,700 copies; and it thus became the only one of my books published prior to 1919 from which the publishers got back the money invested in it.

I cannot conceal from you, though, that the tiny vogue of *The Line of Love* was regrettably brief, nor that the book soon went out of print. It remained in that unhappy and over-populous limbo until November 1921, when a revised version of *The Line of Love* was issued in the Kalki edition. To the text were then added The Wedding Jest and Porcelain Cups, as these tales were composed in the spring of 1919; then in 1928 everything was rewritten yet again for the Storisende edition; and the volume was thus given its present form.

IT HAS always been, rather markedly, the best liked of the four collections of short stories included in the Biography. I do not know why. Yet in revising *The Line of Love* into its final shape, in 1928, I was agreeably astonished by its underlying rationality. I had remembered it as a book compact of all such toplofty romance as was most fashionable in 1905; and I found that, to the contrary, the effect of the whole is just . . . The young people, generation after generation, have each their hour of irresponsibility and of fine language and of preternatural aspirings: then the hour passes: it gives way to more intelligent interests: and, in the long run, the survivors of that glowing hour discover it was not of permanent importance. Yet memory retains the glow and the fervor of it, like a beacon kindled upon once visited heights to which we return no more; so that even nowadays, some of us, now and then, regard its far-off glitter, from a point of view somewhere between the derisory and the embarrassed, with an unreasoned wistfulness.

The High Place

IN *The Line of Love* the Biography has followed the life of Manuel through ten generations, down to its introduction into the Musgrave family. With *The High Place* the tale passes to the sixteenth generation of that life, in a somewhat different line. The Biography now turns again to the gallant race of Puysange.

Raoul de Puysange, whom one encountered in The Conspiracy of Arnaye, removed permanently into England and into some eminence under the first Tudor king, as has already been recorded in *The Line of Love*; but his younger brother, Aristide, remained in France, where he appears in no way particularly to have distinguished himself. It was the son of this Aristide, the Marshal Henri-Jean de Puysange (1493-1555), who rose to some famousness under François the First, and who started the cadet branch of Puysange upon its ascent to power in France,—an ascent so curiously balanced by the decadence, under the name of Pierson, of the older branch in England.

My immediate concern, however, has not ever been with these historical matters. Instead, I aimed, in *The High Place*, to approach a bit more intimately the gallant attitude toward human life. This is the attitude which John Charteris has outlined for you; it is the attitude which Jurgen tested, very provisionally, and upon the whole without committing himself to any verdict. It is, in *The High Place*, the attitude which this second Florian de Puysange attempted: and it is the attitude in which this Florian failed to achieve success. I mean, of course, the first time: for eventually his history had the most happy of endings, in—as it were—an epigeal way.

MEANWHILE I find, in a newspaper symposium printed in the early spring of 1924, wherein various authors explained why he or she had written his or her most recent book, a paragraph under my own name: —

"*The High Place* was written to supply, in my Biography of Manuel's life, the link uniting *The Line of Love* with *Gallantry*. I have therein endeavored, as a needed part of the complete Biography, to illustrate the alternative of Jurgen's choice in the delicate matter of lifting or of leaving untouched the barriers between the material and the ideal. This has been interpreted, perhaps naturally, as an announcing that few wives wear well. I, married, question this construing with great emphasis and discretion . . . And I must likewise, in passing, modestly disclaim all credit, which the illiterate have overgenerously accorded me, for endowing from out of my personal funds of perversity this book's milieu and its social customs: for that these constituents also are plagiarized, anybody can discover who cares to dip into the mildest of the Regency memoirs,—say, of the Duc de Richelieu or even of Saint-Simon."

Yes, that really is, in itself, a sufficient commentary; although this explanation, too, requires a bit of explaining in a world wherein perceptive intelligence is rare . . . It was Florian's fault, then, that he attempted to introduce beauty and holiness into his daily living. It was his error that, when he reached the bedside 'of the sleeping princess, precisely as Jurgen once stood at the bedside of Queen Helen, Florian did not emulate the clinic restraint of his gallant ancestor. Jurgen, you may remember, half drew back the violet coverlet, and then replaced it; and so went away forever blessed with memories, and with no illusion exposed to any possibility of being marred. But Florian raised the coverlet, and awakened the sleeper, with results which *The High Place* commemorates.

Yet later, as you may remember also, Jurgen entered the Heaven of his grandmother, and came face to face with holiness. His conduct in Heaven is upon record: and the fact too is upon record that

Heaven was the second of the places visited by Jurgen from which he went away very hastily,— once more, I must repeat, blessed with his memories, and with no illusion exposed to any possibility of being marred. But Florian had the ill luck to fetch home with him that holiness which thitherto, from an appropriate distance, he had respectfully and lovingly admired.

It thus has occurred naturally to a great many persons that Florian's history is but an enfeebled copy of Jurgen's history, because each is in every respect the exact opposite of the other. Indeed I have always found my circumstances regrettable whensoever the scheme of the Biography involved a return to the same "situation," so as to weigh the result, at this crux, of a different choice by my protagonist—I mean, the life of Manuel—because to so many persons a different solving of the same problem appears, for some obscure reason, to be mere repetition. I regret this. I reflect, in my moments of deeper anguish, that Dickens' *Dombey and Son* and Hergesheimer's *Cytherea* differ from each other in some ways as unmistakably as they do from Homer's *Iliad*, even though all three narratives deal with the elopement of a married woman. But upon the whole I have preferred to work out the Biography rather than the mental quirks of its potential readers.

A word more: I have said it was Florian's fault that he attempted to introduce beauty and holiness

into his daily living. I have written to small purpose
if that statement appears to asperse beauty and holiness. They are fine and, in some sense, they are useful qualities when one adopts either the chivalrous
or the poetic attitude: but with the gallant attitude
they simply and starkly do not blend. It was Florian's
fault that he attempted to combine the incompatible.
The really gallant person accepts the plane of daily
life and makes the best of it: his choice, upon the
whole, is wisdom: but, as any dictionary or as any
portrait of the judiciary of the Supreme Court of the
United States of America will assure you, wisdom
is different from beauty; and more than often is
wisdom at odds with holiness. For wisdom is an
earthly quality: I suspect that its appropriate symbol
is less the owl than the ostrich, who attempts no
flights above earth; who shuts out whatsoever is
dreadful by veiling his gaze with earth; and who
permits nothing on earth to upset his digestion. It
is gratifying to note that Florian de Puysange also,
in the outcome, perceived this incongruity; and that,
with his over-ambitious errors canceled, he lived as a
pattern of the best-thought-of vices, all the long pleasant way to the graveyard, amid the well merited respect of his fellows.

I RETURN to my previously quoted text: to-day it appears droll that in 1923 *The High Place* should have

been regarded as indecent, in that it touches upon sexual eccentricities which were modish during the Orléans Regency. Me that surprised even in 1923, when, as my text points out, the Memoirs of Richelieu and Saint-Simon were in general circulation; and when, for that matter, the letters of Madame Elizabeth Charlotte, the Regent's mother, were enjoying in translation a mild celebrity.

I record here her candid summing up of the day's higher social circles, as addressed to the Duchess of Hanover: "All the young fellows and many of the older ones are so steeped in this vice that they talk of nothing else. Any other form of gallantry is ridiculed; and it is only the common men who make love to women."

Let us not forget that the writer of this frank summary spent some thirty years as the wife of the Sun King's only brother—as the wife of "Monsieur," whose tastes were very especially not those of "common men." During that while she had been favored with hourly opportunities to learn as much about the sports which made Sodom famous as could possibly interest any woman. Madame Elizabeth Charlotte d'Orléans speaks with peculiar authority.

THE writing of *The High Place* was begun in July 1922, during the first visit that I paid to Mountain Lake in Virginia: and the book reveals, they tell

me, sufficing marks of the mountain scenery where-
among this story was begun. It is certain that, when
the book was planned, at Dumbarton, in the early
spring of 1922, the castle of Brunbelois, after the
time-hallowed custom of other enchanted castles,
stood in the low heart of an ancient forest, upon no
elevation at all. But when I began to write out the
tale, under its first title of *The Place That Ought
Not to Be*, it chanced that I too was surrounded by
forests, of quite respectable antiquity, falling away
beneath me as far as the eye could reach: and it presently occurred to me that, through a little editing of
altitudes, I would to all intents be sitting upon the
castle porch in the while that I described Brunbelois,
without ever having to leave my writing table. Sheer
laziness thus prompted me to lift up the castle a mile
or two, to my own physical level; and through the
ever insidious counsels of indolence *The Place That
Ought Not to Be* had become within ten minutes
The High Place.

So was beauty provided with its secret habitation.
For the corresponding high place of holiness I drew
upon my memories of the now deserted and fallen
Rockbridge Alum Springs, to which, if it at all matters, the curious may discover that Upper Morven
bears a remarkable resemblance. And while I was
about this scene shifting, I borrowed from the ruined
Alum lawns that boulder beside which Florian builds
his small fire.

Thereafter, when once the stage was set, the tale flowed on with unusual celerity. This was caused, I think, by the fact that *The High Place* is unique among my writings in possessing a distinct and tolerably symmetrical plot, which, when once set a-going, ran onward of its own momentum to its one logical close. I was at this time naïvely proud of my plot: and I honored it to the extent of not anywhere indulging in the loved pursuit of inserting more or less extraneous matter which happened at that moment to occur to and please my fancy. I thus wasted a great deal of pains and some self-denial, because I do not think that to this date anybody has ever observed that *The High Place* possesses a plot.

The tale was finished in June 1923. It was published the following November, in a first edition of 2000 copies illustrated by Frank C. Papé. The book was re-issued, during the same month, in the unillustrated Kalki edition.

And it "sold" fairly well, in the teeth of the most unanimously abusive press accorded to any of my books. An even half of the reviews, of course, complained that this was *Jurgen* all over again: the remainder regretted that this was by no means another *Jurgen*. But upon the loftier grounds of morality their agreement was general. *The High Place* did not prove, perhaps, quite so individually irritating as *The Cords of Vanity*,—a volume which, for no reason ever known to me, has in each of its several editions revealed in nine out of ten of its reviewers some manifest sense of unprovoked and strong personal injury. But *The High Place* excelled even *The Cords of Vanity* as an awakener of moral reprehension.

And it really does seem rather quaint nowadays . . . The earliest of all reviews, I find, was in the New York *Times*. I record the judicious verdict of Mr. Lloyd Morris: "This book is definitely distasteful in its explicit—and gratuitous—suggestion of sexual aberration and sexual perversion." That in itself was mild enough, and of course would not ever have been written if Mr. Morris at that time had happened to know anything about the Regency period. But the linotypes of half a continent were echoing his sentiments within the week. Then—just as had been the case with that other once salacious volume, *The Eagle's Shadow,*—a fair number of earnest-minded and unliterary persons began to write to their favorite papers to stigmatize *The High Place* as a regrettable instance of what modern literature was coming to.

Brentano's *Book Chat* printed many letters concerning *The High Place*, from standpoints so far diverse (geographically) that I find Mr. R. G. Kirk of Santa Monica, California, lamenting my "stinking filth and vileness" side by side with Mr. E. E. Robinson's petition—as it was transmitted heavenward, through the columns of *Book Chat*, from Pensacola, Florida—that Mr. Robinson's friendly rela-

tions with Jehovah might "never to be besmirched
with the fancies of a distorted brain such as Cabell's."
The New York *Tribune* helpfully suggested, in an
editorial, that the then world-famous Leopold-Loeb
murder had been prompted by a reading of *The
High Place*. I personally was favored with much un-
solicited correspondence, of a comminatory nature,
which in no half-sentence honored the sedate Postal
Regulations of a Christian democracy. And for the
rest, I find that even the very lateliest dated of the
reviews of *The High Place* now in my scrapbook—a
review written by H. W. A., for the Akron (Ohio)
Press—is regrettably of a piece with its hundred or
so predecessors, in affirming, "*The High Place* is an
utterly impossible, sacrilegious, immoral and obscene
work that could not be too strongly condemned."

—Upon which note I close, in deep and honest
sadness; for it really is dejecting to observe how soon,
how inexpressibly soon—in what humiliating trices
and sardonic twinklings of Time's eye—does the
very loftiest rhetoric, if it be envenomed with moral
indignation, go out of date. That seems always to
happen when (as John Milton phrases it) a cool un-
passionate mildness is not enough to damp and aston-
ish the wicked, and when "the invincible warrior
Zeal" is thus forced to adopt other measures, vo-
ciferously. It is then that Milton himself splutters
in his only too well justified wrath at the goings-on
of such rogues as Smectymnuus and Salmasius; that

the finest sensibilities of John Wilson Croker are nauseated by a Cockney Keats, popped out of a chemist shop to assault Helicon; that Demosthenes lays bare the un-Athenian iniquities of King Philip; and that Isaiah, both of him, regards without any approval the civic morals of Babylon.

Well, and it all seems tremendously important, at the time, sounding as a heart-stirring trumpet which calls upon human virtue to defend its ideals. Yet somehow, even in the aforementioned trices and twinklings, these noble voices are stilled rather dreadfully soon. The special fashion of their altruism is outmoded. Cold type alone records their magnanimous ardors, in a shrivelled sour parody. And the unanswerableness of their logic is quite forgotten except by a few sporadic and not really interested persons who at times mildly wonder just what, after all, the remote rumpus was about, precisely?

Gallantry

ONLY too many of our most imposing words seem but too rarely ever to get out of the dictionary. There is, for example, "mundicidious,"—which means, of course, "happening in the present world." That is the word which suggests itself now that I come to consider *Gallantry*.

This volume, as the life of Manuel passes onward into the bodies of that seventeenth generation which immediately followed the generation of Florian de Puysange, is concerned in particular with the gallant attitude of a number of persons who, without ascending any unwholesomely high places, accepted their casual surroundings, and who made, from any mundane point of view, the best of them. This volume, thus, approaches yet again, but from another angle, a theme explained in earlier volumes, as well as in this special volume's Epistle Dedicatory—which goes boldly to the affair's heart.

It follows that this *Gallantry* remains, throughout, very resolutely superficial. Each one of the persons dealt with in *Gallantry* accepted his, or it might

be her, terrestrial surroundings without really bothering about the inner being of himself or of herself,
or of his or her companions, or about any other
matters either above or below his (or it might be
her) chance-assigned orbit in life. These people, in
fine, were worldlings, although not necessarily in an
ignoble sense of the word: and so this volume of the
Biography differs from all the preceding volumes in
that the concerns of this particular stage in the journeying of Manuel's life from one generation to another are frankly mundicidious.

I SHALL here confess that in editing for the Storisende
edition the work of that comparative stranger who
had written *Gallantry* a good while over twenty
years earlier, I found pleasure now and then in the
literary style of Captain Audaine, a moderate sympathy with Louis de Soyecourt, and a real liking for
Ormskirk. I do not, heaven be my witness, regard
Ormskirk with quite the eyes of the young man who
first involved Ormskirk in the Biography. I suspect,
indeed, an error somewhere in the computations of
this young man, for I profoundly doubt that his
Ormskirk is forty-five years old. Nevertheless there
is, to my indulgent fancy, some life in Ormskirk.
And I would incline also to applaud, as being neat
craftsmanship, the steadily varying aspect in which

the plump Duke is presented to the reader if only I
did not happen to remember that this technical nicety
was contrived by no writer, but by accident. In any
case, the character whom I view nowadays with the
most lively interest is no one of the three I have
named.

I recall Hugh Walpole's bland question after
he had read this book—a question which of course
was tendered in Hugh's habitual manner, of a kindly
hearted bishop examining a candidate for confirma-
tion,—"But what was it, James, that you first planned
to do with Vanringham?" That question did not seem
inevitable. It was answered with I forget what vague
mendacity. But the question showed that, to the eye
of the trained novelist, here in this *Gallantry* was
apparent a forsaken intention, and the wreckage of a
lost battle which had left traces of more than the
book anywhere divulged. For Francis Vanringham
was, as I privately knew, the most important of all
my characters in the bud, as it were, and masked
with an alias.

This *Gallantry* is everywhere a book of begin-
nings. Poictesme began with *Gallantry*, as is explained in another place. With Ormskirk began the
first sketching of that afterward omnipresent person
whom Mr. Thomas Beer has described as "the talka-
tive Northern lover, the broken idealist of women."
And Horvendile also began with *Gallantry*,—

wherein, as you may have guessed, he wears the name
of Francis Vanringham.

For, when I returned again to the legends of
Allonby and of the cadet branch of the race of
Puysange, I made a queer discovery as to that Francis Vanringham who figured in the affairs of both
houses just after the middle of the eighteenth century. And it was my notion, at first, to let Vanringham
play a more and ever more prominent part in *Gallantry* until, toward the end—in that extraordinary
scene which Löwe records—this Vanringham should
be revealed as the Author who had planned and
guided all. I did not mean to adopt Löwe's explanation that Vanringham was insane.

But the young fellow who wrote *Gallantry* in 1905
could not quite manage that planned *coup* . . . The
trouble was, as I now know, that any prominence
at all is incompatible with omnipotence. It is necessary, for a reason never yet made clear to me, that
in his own work every Author should be restrained
to an apparently minor part.

This rule of thumb, adhered to by all demiurges,
I did not discover, though, until 1914, when *The
Cream of the Jest* was being written. It was only
then that, under the guidance of Richard Harrowby,
I took up, in a more or less serious way, the study
of what is loosely called "magic," and that I learned
something of those realities which are behind what
we, just as loosely, call "ordinary experience." It

was only then, in fine, that I turned definitely away from the merely mundicidious.

MEANWHILE it seems fairly obvious that this Horvendile, lurking to the back of my mind just beyond my actual consciousness, had tried rather hard to get into *Domnei*, where the part appears rightfully his which is played by Ahasuerus; and that the attempt was foiled by my then inadequate comprehension of Horvendile.

In the time that I was completing *Gallantry*, I found Vanringham complaisant enough in aiding me to, in an ever-useful phrase, a certain extent. But beyond that, it seemed, this Vanringham would not go. He would accept no earthly pre-eminence. Prod and remodel as I might, it appeared that this scant penny's worth of ink and paper was, in some way, a person who obstinately sought out a semi-obscurity for himself; he was a person not upon any terms to be coerced by the needs of my intended "plot"; and in preference to ending as the brightest ornament to Ormskirk's dinner table in the Afterpiece this Vanringham, so far as I could determine, quite indissuadably elected to wind up this particular incarnation as a valet in an inn-parlor.

I deal, I imagine, with an experience fairly common to most writers. The puppets now and then turn refractory; and in an insanely matter-of-fact way

convince you that what really happened to them was
wholly different from what you have laboriously
caused to happen to them . . . In Vanringham, at
all events, I found no variability nor any shadow of
turning as he passed casually through what I wrote
about him, with an odd air of discovering himself at
loose ends in the wrong book and of being unfrettedly
intent to get out of it as soon as possible.

Then, in *The Cream of the Jest*, I foregathered
with Richard Harrowby. I report his findings without—as heaven again knows—endorsing them. It
was Dick Harrowby's notion that the Author, that
nameless Author whose work in the Biography I
was attempting to record, preferred to remain a
subordinate character in the romances which He contrived and guided,—somewhat as Shakespeare appeared as Adam in *As You Like It*, or as Christ
figured as a carpenter's son in the most backward
district of a minor Roman province, or as Odin the
All-Father was accustomed to wander among his
human playthings in the seeming of an aged, one-
eyed, out-at-elbows and wholly inconsiderable vagabond. I willy-nilly must humor the Author who had
in charge the life of Manuel, if I indeed was to go
on with my transcription of the Biography.

Such were the findings of Richard Harrowby;
no doubt they were nonsense. Yet it is a fact that
under this illogical one sole restriction all did henceforward work out more glibly. Horvendile, upon

these terms, did actually come more and more fully
into the field of my consciousness; and he even permitted me to disclose that from the first he had been
Vanringham, as the curious may discover in the fif-
teenth chapter of *The Cream of the Jest.* Was he
also Ahasuerus, that ever-living being with no superhuman trait except immortality? that undivine immortal whose existence is everywhere reported in
folk-lore, and is but very inadequately explained by
blurred legends about the Flying Dutchman and the
Peripatetic Episcopalian and El Khoudr and the
Wandering Jew? That I do not know: and I decline
here to nurture any speculations which aim beyond
the mundicidious.

YET we have the word of Freydis for it, that very
often, just for the sport's sake, do the people of
Audela go among us in the likeness of mere mortal
men and women. It has occurred to me, too, that the
word Audela is suggestively similar to Ydalir, whence
Koshchei came. But I would not press this point. I
prefer upon the whole to regard the similarity as an
unmeaning coincidence: and I draw from it no deduction whatever.

Nor has it really hampered me in completing the
Biography, that I do not, and cannot hope to, understand Horvendile. I do not understand Manuel
either. It seems natural enough that these two alone

—who represent the origin of all the life in the Biography and the power which guides this life— should remain unexplained. The other characters have been made to me, each in turn, quite comprehensible. Nor does it matter that I may not understand the origin of the long drama of the life of Manuel, nor who guides it toward what end, but can appraise only the costumes in the way of human bodies which this life assumes and casts by during its unpredictable journeying. It is so with my own life, and with the life of every person who is not too utterly an addict of the drug called use and wont. All springs from, as all travels toward, mystery. It is so with all human life, which everywhere is bound in by transient superficies behind which move perceptibly the unseen and the inapprehensible.

It is so, I suspect, with the life of Horvendile, whether it be in Audela or in Ydalir or in some yet other country that, in seeking diversion from the monotonous surface and the underlying uneasiness of his inexplicable daily existence, he seeks to create and to play with the inheritors of Manuel's life. And it is so, we are given to understand, with that demiurge who shaped and populated our own planet. At least I am aware of no cosmogony which does not postulate a deity, mildly bored with the round of his normal existence, who created men and women in his search of diversion. All creation is the result of boredom: that is the first tenet of all art and of every known religion.

Yet as to these high matters I have no desire to become dogmatic. I very heartily know that these matters are none of my responsibility, nor my concern, as yet, anyhow. . . . So is it that we come back to the starting point. Our own Horvendile, by whatsoever name you may elect to call Him, stays unexplained. If He indeed created us after His own image, it is yet the part of optimism to reflect that He may be one of those artists who do not excel at catching a likeness. Meanwhile I do not know but that each one of us would wiseliest, after the fine example of the fribbles in this book called *Gallantry*, make the best of his or her surroundings, without bothering overmuch about any matters below or above his or her special orbit in life. Our immediate concerns are, as yet, mundicidious.

THE first written of these stories was The Ducal Audience, done in September 1901. Two more of them—Love at Martinmas and The Rhyme to Porringer—were written during the following December. Heart of Gold came next, in November 1902. But it was not until the autumn of 1904 that the volume began to take definite shape in my mind, nor until the spring of 1905 that I had my useless struggle with Vanringham. From this I retired defeated.

I decided to leave the unmanageable red-head prostrate upon the floor of the Golden Pomegranate in Manneville; and when in imagination I returned to Tunbridge Wells, during the autumn of 1905, I promoted his grace of Ormskirk to be the leading man in this *Gallantry*. During my first mental rehearsals of *Gallantry* John Bulmer had been cast as but little more than a supernumerary. The book was then virtually completed in 1905,—although the lateliest done of the stories, The Scapegoats (wherein at long last I disposed of Vanringham) did not get written until February 1906.

Meanwhile all the tales except one had found hospitality in various magazines. . . . The Rhyme to Porringer, after having been rather widely rejected, was entered in the Collier's prize contest for 1905. It, naturally, did not win the $5000 prize, which was carried off by Mr. Rowland Thomas, with a tale called Fagan: but The Rhyme to Porringer was placed as the thirteenth in merit among the various entrants, and so was purchased for the highest price which I had ever received for a story. I was paid $200.75; and until the date of my decease I shall continue to wonder upon what principle this odd total was worked out. . . . But In the Second April I could sell nowhere: and, after it had knocked about for a year and a half, it was still undisposed of in May 1906, when Harper & Brothers accepted the complete book *Gallantry* for publication.

It was then suggested to me that this yet-unsold
In the Second April was well suited to the requirements of *Harper's Monthly Magazine*; and that this
periodical would be pleased to purchase it. There
seemed no pressing need for me to object that this
magazine, in common with nearly every other magazine in the country, had already rejected this story.
So I consented, amicably enough, to sell the serial
rights of In the Second April; and it duly appeared
in *Harper's Monthly Magazine*, some six months
before *Gallantry* was published, on 10 October 1907.

Inasmuch as its predecessor, *The Line of Love*,
had "sold" acceptably, I regarded *Gallantry* with
hopes not unmercantile. But all students of archæ-
ology will comprehend that no book published upon
10 October 1907 had a fair chance of success. Hardly
had *Gallantry* been put in the market when, on 22
October 1907, the Knickerbocker Trust Company
failed; the Electric & Manufacturing Company forthwith went into the hands of receivers; and in New
York City alone, one national bank, four trust companies, and six state banks, promptly closed their
doors. Currency then rose, I am told, to a premium
of 4½%; and money, where it could be obtained at
all, was lent at 125%. In fine, there occurred that
which, to the naïve inexperience of 1907, appeared
a financial panic.

In such circumstances nobody wasted money upon
reading-matter. Virtually no books were sold that

autumn, they tell me, with the exception of Elinor Glyn's masterwork, *Three Weeks*—whose exceeding wickedness continued to lead prurience into triumphing over thrift. Against the competition and the satanic iniquities of a love-affair conducted—as it was even hinted, recumbently—on a tiger-skin rug, *Gallantry* had no least chance. So in the October of 1907 *Gallantry* failed as completely as though it had been a large brokerage firm.

It was therefore permitted to go out of print for the next fifteen years, but it was republished in 1922, in the Kalki edition, when some of the more highly romantic passages, in the very best taste of 1907, were mercifully omitted. Yet later *Gallantry* was rewritten for the Storisende edition; and upon this occasion the general trend of the whole book was made yet further—as one might say—mundicidious.

Something About Eve

I T MAY be recalled that in *The Line of Love* the
life of Manuel was traced through some three
centuries of journeying, down to the introduction of
that life into the Musgrave family; and that there
the Biography paused, temporarily, because the history of all the Musgrave descendants is elsewhere
recorded, in *The Musgraves of Matocton*, with tolerable completeness. You may read also in *The
Musgraves of Matocton* (p. 205) of how, in 1773,
the daughter of that same Gerald Allonby concerning whom you have heard somewhat in *Gallantry*
eloped from Torwood Manor with her remote kins-
man, Theodorick Quentin Musgrave, then the lineal
head of the American Musgraves. Now it is with
their eldest son that the Biography deals in *Something About Eve,*—with that Gerald Musgrave to
whom, alike through his father and his mother, the
life of Manuel was thus transmitted in the nineteenth
generation.

About this Gerald Musgrave I have made a book
for two main reasons. He alone of all the American

Musgraves had a career of which *The Musgraves of Matocton*, in its leisured dalliance with dates and legislative services and epitaphs and war records, speaks no word. It speaks instead of Glaum's scholastic career in the body of Gerald Musgrave. My second reason is that this Gerald, alone of the American Musgraves, adopted toward life, howsoever bunglingly, the poetic attitude, concerning which John Charteris and I have already remarked somewhat more than suffices.

For now, in this tenth volume, the Biography reverts to the clan of old Madoc, who was neither chivalrous nor gallant, but merely a poet,—a never-idle "maker"; and to whom all human life afforded, in the ultimate, only the raw materials which his half-tranced imaginings might remake into something more comely, more symmetrical, and more diverting. Gerald Musgrave alone of the sober-minded Musgraves was of this clan. Gerald Musgrave turned inevitably, neglecting all else, toward this or that rather beautiful idea to play with. And the history of Gerald Musgrave, therefore, sets forth how he failed, as most and perhaps all poets fail, to reach Antan.

YOU have already seen, in the commentary upon *The High Place*, with what diffidence, inasmuch as nobody appeared to perceive that *The High Place* possessed a rounded and jealously ordered plot, I myself was compelled to point out the fact. Here arises an even less graceful necessity. *The High Place* was so liberally assailed, it was so mauled and clapperclawed and spewed at, that its perpetrator might feel privileged by decorum, in mere self-defence, to dwell upon such subaltern merits as the book appeared to him, even so, to display. But *Something About Eve* fared more happily. It was abused in a moderate number of not at all moderate reviews, of course, for being indecent, and for being a repetition of *Jurgen*, and for not being a repetition of *Jurgen*; but that was to be expected, irrespective of the book's contents. . . . I remember too that Henry Seidel Canby, of the *Literary Review*, thought poorly of this book at some length: but almost immediately Dr. Canby was out with an article in which he ranked his assistant editor, Mr. Christopher Morley, with Goethe and Shakespeare, and thus made Mr. Morley and myself feel quite comfortable. . . . So, upon the whole, *Something About Eve* was favorably treated. And I have no valid complaint to advance about its reception as merchandise.

Yet one discovers, in looking over the hundreds of reviews accorded to *Something About Eve*, a fact which does seem mildly disconcerting: it is the sad fact that no literary critic, and, so far as I know, not any reader, evinced the least glimmering of perception as to what was the book's theme and object.

TO BE sure, the Washington (D. C.) *Post* did raise this exact question, and did settle it, at least to the reviewer's satisfaction, in a manner so succinct that the entire review may here be quoted:

"The author could have had but one object in writing this book,—to prove that a book of about 350 pages can be written without containing a single idea. He calls it a 'Comedy of Fig Leaves.' A comedy implies some humor, but there is no humor in this book. There is nothing about Eve, and nothing about fig leaves, either materially or metaphorically."

That is all which the *Post* had to say as to *Something About Eve*. Yet I do not think that this summary, howsoever candid, is wholly true. Nor do I think the more general finding—that *Something About Eve* concerns man's aspirations as they are at first hampered, and at last foiled, by his woman-kind—to come very much nearer to the book's actual theme than did the Washington (D. C.) *Post*.

TO MY mind, it is sometimes plain that Gerald's failure to reach Antan was caused by no woman's beguilements. What detained him, when there remained no impediment between him and his goal, I would suggest to have been, perhaps, his own nature. Here are the woman and the child and common cordial human living: yonder in Antan is but ambiguity, it may be very glorious, it may be merely lethal. All

news as to Antan, let it be pointed out, comes always
to Gerald Musgrave from sources rather more than
suspect. Meanwhile, here, upon Mispec Moor, stays
that which is familiar and most dear. Man—being
what he is—requires no persuading to remain where
love attends him. The gods and the great myths go
by, toward, it may be, concerns which are more lofty
and more magnanimous: but man remains, of his
own choice, and, be it added, because of all the wisdom that living has ever taught him.

There are, it is said, those exceptional men who
adventure very gloriously into Antan. Yet this
rumor, too, comes always from ambiguous sources.
It is merely certain that in the while of Gerald's tar-
rying with his Maya no human being, of either sex,
went beyond Mispec Moor. And, in Gerald's case at
least, it seems fairly certain also that not Maya
detained her husband within arm's reach of the goal
of all the gods of men, but the lucky fact that upon
Mispec Moor Gerald Musgrave had found what
contented his nature. There was not any need to
journey farther.

Antan remains, they say, the home of all true
poets. Yet no man is entirely a poet. A part of him
is a husband, a part is a father, for example; and
with these considerable fractions of a man's being,
Antan has no concern, and Antan proffers to them
no allure. It results that, although, as even a myopic
Rossetti has observed, so many men are poets in

their youth, yet, with age, and with the accompanying growth in complexity of each man's nature, all men, and most certainly all avowed poets, fail more or less completely as poets. I would but point out that to fail as a poet may very well be to succeed as a human being. Gerald did not reach Antan: yet he gained, so far as he could discover, the most nearly satisfying prizes which human life affords. He, in any case, was not ever so discourteous as to blame upon any woman the outcome that he attained to no more: and I conjecture that you and I may with profit emulate him in chivalry. . . . Instead, the enemy was within: and instead, for all that I know, the enemy turned out, in the end, to have been a benefactor,—within of course those brief and not over-fertile fields wherein beneficence, howsoever fleetingly, touches human living.

—None of which may be true, to be sure: I would but suggest that now and then this appears, in Gerald's favorite phrase, a rather beautiful idea to play with.

THIS book was begun I dare not say how many years before its completion. I appear to have no note as to exactly when *Something About Eve* was started; but it was put aside in 1918, in order that I might write *Jurgen*. Thus *Something About Eve* was already an ageing and much interlined manuscript when, in 1923,

Guy Holt compiled his Bibliography of my writings, and in that opus duly listed *Something About Eve* among my forthcoming works. The chief difference between the present book and the form which this tale retained for years was that, in the earlier version, the story passed straightway from Gerald's departure from out of human living to his meeting with Maya. There was, that is, in the earlier version nothing corresponding to Chapters V-XXII, but instead only a gap which I meant by-and-by to fill in, and which I never did bridge over in the tale's first form. Nor did the missing matter then appear especially important, because to me the real theme was always just the story of Gerald's contented stay upon Mispec Moor, with the gods and the myths of men passing onward to an ambiguous fate which he elected not to provoke for himself.

In any event, I became dissatisfied with the tale, for one reason and another, and the manuscript of the first version was burned in the spring of 1925. Gerald Musgrave seemed now at one with his near kinswomen, Wilhelmina Musgrave and Cynthia Musgrave, and with Hugh de Lusignan, and with George Bulmer, whose partially completed histories had all ended in the hall fireplace at Dumbarton Grange: and I turned to *The Silver Stallion*, and afterward to *The Music from Behind the Moon*. Yet all the while this red-headed Gerald Musgrave, whom I had first met in the pages of *The Rivet in*

Grandfather's Neck, retained an obscure footing in the very back of my mind. Thence he, as one who foreknows the outcome, appeared to regard me with an air of amiable and humorous mockery which became more and yet more familiar. Meanwhile that ruthless bust of Æsred which Edmond Amateis had made for me, out of a bit of marble from Nero's Golden House, stayed in my writing-room: and she too appeared to regard me with a sort of sullen expectation. The two of them, in fine, seemed bent upon my writing *Something About Eve.*

So I came back to Gerald Musgrave, after all, in the July of 1926. I found, in Cayford Cottage, just such a cottage as Gerald inhabited; I found, in appraising the vista from the porch of that cottage, a fair duplicate of Antan, in the remote appearance of Pembroke, Virginia; and I found too that Gerald Musgrave's life history had become very easy to write. There was, now, no difficulty whatever about it. Now, the tale flowed onward without a stop,— with Nero sauntering into the story, as an affair of course,—and it seemed rather to complete itself, at last, in the June of 1927. I do not assert that this is the best of my books: but I am sure it received more thinking about than any of the others, inasmuch as this tale was in my mind for some ten years; and I am sure, too, that, after the first draft had been destroyed and everything begun all over again, this *Something About Eve* is the story which I wrote with

the most liberal allotment of ease and pleasure. Of
the many characters in the Biography I have found
Gerald Musgrave the most companionable.

Something About Eve was published in September
1927. To my chief collaborator was then paid the
tribute of illustrating the large paper edition with a
picture of that bust of Æsred which had both chap-
eroned and allured me through the book's writing.

But again I found that, as had been the case with
Figures of Earth, so here my first conception of
Something About Eve seemed in the completed book
to have been obscured beyond human discovery. To
me this was always the story of Gerald's stay upon
Mispec Moor: to a troublingly large number of my
readers, I found, it was, instead, the story of Gerald's
journeying toward Mispec Moor, and of his adventuring with Evadne and Evasherah and Evarvan and
Evaine, to which all the latter half of the book figured as a relatively unimportant epilogue. And I find,
to this day, that notion is prevalent.

Now there are several ways of explaining this.
One is, that the material with which I finally filled
in the years-old gap in Gerald's history happened,
somehow, to be superior in quality to the remainder
of the book, which corresponds to the story as I first
shaped it. Of that possibility I am no judge. A rather

less flattering explanation is, that few readers got farther than the middle of the book.

But I think this shift in emphasis is, rather, to be accounted for by the fact that to the immature-minded any reference to sexual matters is impressive beyond its rational weight. Given a book in which there is one hint of the technically "indecent," it is that single passage which the mentally immature, howsoever staid and gray, will remember, whether with sniggers or with indignation, long after the rest of the book is forgotten.

I recall a queer instance of this in the reception accorded to Hugh Walpole's at one time widely read book, *The Young Enchanted,* in which novel a four-letter word, thitherto—to purloin a phrase from George Jean Nathan—"more intimately associated with latrines than with literature," occurred just once, and promptly became the pivot of any general discussion of *The Young Enchanted.* More lately, I remember, the famousness of William Faulkner has grown from one corn-cob. And I reflect also that while to-day the translated texts of Rabelais and of Apuleius and of the *Decameron* and of Suetonius are customarily printed in full, the sole passages actually read therein by the most of us are those passages which in my boyhood remained "veiled in the obscurity of a learned language."

From these noticeably divergent instances of the importance which the immature-minded attach to any and all sorts of "indecency," I deduce it is natural enough that to many of my readers *Something About Eve* must appear to be an account of Gerald Musgrave's temptation by various women, and of his edifying resistance to their carnality. I admire the moral, which has two edges. Nevertheless does candor compel me to repeat that, so far as I am concerned, this book relates the history of Gerald Musgrave's resting upon Mispec Moor, to his ruin as a practising poet, but to his enlargement as a human being.

The Certain Hour

THE Biography turns now to those inheritors of Dom Manuel's life to whom the Biography has made many earlier references. I mean, the ten images which Manuel shaped upon Upper Morven; which Niafer regarded unfavorably at Sargyll; and to which Freydis, after her removal into Antan, gave human life, for the reasons that in *The High Place* she explained to Florian de Puysange. In *The Certain Hour* you have some account of how these ten sped in a world which seemed not wholly native, because each of these ten, although fashioned of terrestrial clay, was informed with the fire of Audela, and because to each of them life had first been given in Antan,—in that Antan from which their existence among men was perforce a sort of exile.

Moreover, in this volume, the Biography concerns yet again the poetic attitude toward life. It was the attitude in which Gerald Musgrave failed, and in which these ten may be said to have succeeded—provided always that one regards success from the unhuman standpoint of an Economist.

146

WE TOUCH here the perplexing question raised by the progenitor of all my characters, and solved, so far as I can perceive, by none of them. "Ah, but," said Manuel, "what is success?" By Gerald, who failed as a poet, was gained, upon the whole, success as a human being: he had his thirty honored years of untroubled living, upon Mispec Moor, among the wholesome surroundings of a contented home life. He had, again upon the whole, the most nearly satisfying lot attainable by mankind. But he himself created nothing permanent,—whereas the ethnological tomes which had been compiled by his natural body all fared as do all scientific books which are empoisoned with temporarily sound and valuable information, in that they soon went out of date and were forgotten: moreover, Gerald did not attain to Antan.

Now the ten with whom we deal in *The Certain Hour* all more or less brilliantly succeeded according to the criteria which in *Beyond Life* John Charteris has outlined in talking about the Economist. Yet as human beings no one of them might be ranked as successful. They created, each in his fashion, that which was fairly permanent: but they themselves were native to Antan rather than to the world of that human race among whom they fared as changelings. More or less vividly they remembered always, I think, their native, far-away Antan: and that memory kept the surroundings which were immediately about

them always a bit unsatisfying. In brief, they lived
as poets; and all poets, until Time and Conformity
have subdued them into rational human beings, must
live as exiles.

This book commemorates, as I would have you
bear in mind, but a single hour from the terrestrial
exile of each of these ten Manuelites. With Herrick,
and with Pope, and with Ufford, it was no merry
hour. And indeed I find that, with a depressing regu-
larity, the others of my ten, each one of them, howsoever cheerily they may figure in this book, came
by-and-by to no desirable ending. Raimbaut de Va-
queiras and Shakespeare were already spent: so that
each, after his portrayed hour, unostentatiously and
briefly flickered out of living, like lamps in which
there is no more oil. Alessandro de Medici and John
Charteris were murdered, each more or less justi-
fiably. And Wycherley and Sheridan, after their
abandonment of the desire to write perfectly of beautiful happenings, sped steadily downward—sharing
meanwhile no happy living with the wives whom in
this book they acquire merrily,—and so came, before
winning the delayed mercy of death, to squalor and
imbecility.

Vanderhoffen alone, under the loving despotism
of his capable wife, reached a well-thought-of late
middle age, as a superior hack writer; and then
marred a fine common-sense moral by going insane,
just as Wycherley and Sheridan had done before him,

after they also had pawned their birthrights for one or another genteel sort of pottage . . . We can but deduce that the lives of those who are touched with the fire of Audela, and who are teased with never dying memories of Antan, are not upon the whole the lives of successful human beings. And the true moral of this account of triumphant Economy would thus seem to be voiced fairly enough in the story called Judith's Creed,—"Lord, what a deal of ruined life it takes to make a little art!"

So much appears needed to explain the place of *The Certain Hour* in the complete Biography. The individual aspects of this volume are sufficiently dealt with, I believe, in its Auctorial Induction,—a piece of writing to which the many changes in literary affairs since 1916 have lent a wholly unpremeditated archæological value.

THE earliest of these stories, Olivia's Pottage, was written—in its first form and under another title— in October 1907. Belhs Cavaliers followed in the December of the same year. The series was then put aside for precisely two years, until when, in December 1909, was written Pro Honoria.

During 1910 were finished, at Richmond-in-Virginia, Judith's Creed, The Irresistible Ogle, Concerning Corinna, and A Princess of Grub Street, in the order given. The year 1911 added nothing to this

dizain. But in the autumn of 1912, in West Virginia,
I returned to *The Certain Hour*, and wrote succes-
sively The Lady of All Our Dreams, A Brown
Woman, and Balthazar's Daughter.

Meanwhile I could do woefully little with these
stories in the inhospitable haunts of magazine editors. *Harper's Monthly Magazine* had accepted
Olivia's Pottage in October 1907,—chiefly, as I now
know, because during the preceding spring the magazine had commissioned me to do "another new story."
Harper's Monthly Magazine did not really want
any more of my stories now that Howard Pyle objected to illustrating them.

Later the *Red Book* bought A Princess of Grub
Street. But the other tales proved everywhere "un-
available." It required a liberal deal of wasted post-
age and of the proverbial hope deferred before I
could sell, finally, another one of them; but, in October 1912, I did succeed in bartering The Lady of
All Our Dreams for eighteen dollars. And by-and-
by, in the spring of 1913, the *Smart Set* accepted
Balthazar's Daughter . . . Thus the matter rested.
If there existed in the United States of America any
fiction-buying magazine which had not definitely rejected the other six stories, it was merely because I
did not have the address of that publication.

In the mean time the book as a whole had been
finished, at Branchland in West Virginia, upon the
then uncultured banks of the Guyan river: and on

the opening day of December 1912 the complete
text of *The Certain Hour* was expressed to Richmond-in-Virginia, so that my combined manuscript
and tyro typing might all be typed out in a fair copy
wherewith to woo book publishers. That came very
near being the last of *The Certain Hour*.

MY PARCEL seems to have arrived in Richmond on
the evening of 3 December 1912. It was during this
night that the building then occupied by the Adams
& Southern Express Company, at Ninth and Cary
Streets, was destroyed by fire. An adjacent building,
then housing the Virginia School Supply Company,
also was ignited disastrously; so that there was a
total loss of some $110,000. But I am afraid that all
other damages involved seemed to me trivial when
I learned, as I soon did, that the only existent copy
of *The Certain Hour* had reached Richmond precisely in time to be burned with the express company's building. Of three stories only, out of the ten
stories, had I another copy. All else was gone.

This was not cheering news for me to be receiving
in West Virginia, because, howsoever lightly all
magazine editors tended to evaluate these tales, it
appeared ungratifying to lose seven of them overnight. I was not happy for the next week. Then came
surprising and more cheerful information. When the
building collapsed, a few parcels had either been

stored in, or else had fallen through into, the cellar.
They had lain there, while the fires above them
burned out; and these parcels had been duly found,
in a more or less scorched or water-soaked condition,
after the ruins of the burned building had been
cleared away. The Adams & Southern Express Company therefore took great pleasure in returning to
me the typescript of my book, of which only the
wrapper and outer pages had been lost. That was
the consolatory news which I now received; and a
bit later came the package.

I have no doubt that my fingers were a little tremu-
lous when I unwrapped the parcel; but I was wholly
pleased by the quasi-miracle. It bespoke a fine fair-
ness on the part of Providence.

Only, I at once discovered that the miracle was
continuing. *The Certain Hour* had been so trans-
muted through its misadventures by fire and water
that hardly any word in it remained unchanged. Even
the title of *The Certain Hour* had perceptibly altered. It was now called *My Seven Husbands*. In
brief, the book typescript thus happily protected by
divine Providence, and replevined by the express
company, displayed, over and above the scars of its
rough usage, the fault of being a typescript which I
had not ever seen before that gray ghastly morning.
It was the unskilled, laborious typing—performed,
no doubt, after my own fashion, entirely with the
right-hand fore-finger—of some other imbecile who

wanted to write books. And I could not but wonder
how fate, as a self-respecting abstraction, could have
sunk to any such unfair favoritism as not to have
burned up *My Seven Husbands* at least seven times in
preference to burning up my book.

Let us not go into the planet-struck, long correspondence which followed. The express company
was polite, but upon the whole unsympathetic. I had
lost a book typescript, and I had got back a book
typescript. Wherein, after that, my grievance could
possibly lodge, the express company, I gathered, did
not perceive. In fact, since the typescript which I now
had was considerably the longer, I had gained by
the transaction.

It may be, of course, that during the year or so
which has elapsed since 1912 I have forgotten a detail
or two, here and there, but I am sure this was the
general attitude of my several correspondents, all
whom were connected officially with the Adams &
Southern Express Company. They were fending off,
quite naturally, any potential claim for damages.
And I, since no one else had ever seen the text of
The Certain Hour, possessed no least legal proof
that the fore-finger which had not over neatly typed
My Seven Husbands was not my own fore-finger.

So did it come about that, throughout the December of 1912 and the January of 1913, the multi-
farious Agents of innumerable Departments—with
that stereotyped official politeness which assumes as

a matter of course your dishonesty without ever actually mentioning it—every one of them adhered to the sturdy common-sense point of view that a book typescript was a book typescript, and that after the misdemeanor of writing *My Seven Husbands*, I was now bent upon the crime of swindling the Adams & Southern Express Company out of twenty dollars. And I learned too, at this season, that it is not ever really profitable to attempt to engage an express company in a discussion of such literary niceties as the difference between one book and another book. Such fine-drawn distinctions do not deeply interest the officials of an express company; and to stress these idle topics can evoke at best only a civilly worded reminder that, if you will but stop being unreasonable and face your begrimed past with more honestness, you will recall having written *My Seven Husbands*.

Then, at the very bottom of the charred wreckage at Ninth and Cary Streets, was found the parcel containing *The Certain Hour*—a little damp, but to every practical intent not hurt at all. After some six weeks, and a Christmas rather strikingly devoid of peace and good will, I was thus permitted to relinquish the enforced authorship of *My Seven Husbands*, and to exchange typescripts with the express company. Even so, the last Agent to write me was clearly of the opinion that I was lucky to get out of this affair without open detection, and that for the future I had better be more careful.

NOR did I appear to have gained anything by having retrieved *The Certain Hour* from its six weeks' stay in the bowels of a dead conflagration. If magazine editors had regarded these stories one by one without any enthusiasm, I now discovered that the admiration which these tales in their collected form aroused among book publishers was equally calm. I appear to have no record as to who rejected *The Certain Hour* in 1913; but the eleven firms who would have none of it in 1914 are all despairingly listed; and I find that I have, too, their disclamatory notes concerning *The Certain Hour*.

Most of these notes are frank as to the book's worthlessness. Here, for example, is Mr. George Haven Putnam writing, for G. P. Putnam's Sons, with at least the generosity of two b's in "Cabbell," that "these stories do not possess the commanding interest which would give them any right to exist in the crowded market for fiction." Mr. Mitchell Kennerley, speaking for himself Incorporated, raises no very differently worded elegy over abortive aspirations. And Mr. Roland Holt, in the full royal mourning of a purple signature stamp, as Vice-President of Henry Holt and Company, after lamenting the decrease in attractiveness between this book and its

author's earlier writings, is of the opinion that "you
have not done effective work in it, and it is not effective enough to make its way." Nor can I find that
any other of these rejectors wrote otherwise than
from very much the point of view of an Agent for
an express company . . . They were acting with
wisdom, of course, as the event proved. Yet I did not
really comprehend, in those days, the shrinking, the
almost panic abhorrence with which every publisher
regards any volume of short stories.

Harpers had brought out my short stories in book
form solely through the hope that Howard Pyle's
pictures might make the book salable: and this hope
had failed, leaving everywhere in all book stores the
gaudy proofs of its wreckage. *The Soul of Melicent*
at that season was conspicuous upon the "remainder"
counters marked down to nineteen cents,—along with
many copies of *Gallantry* and of *Chivalry* more aspiringly priced at fifty cents, and of *The Cords of
Vanity* and of *The Eagle's Shadow* at the judicious
compromise of a quarter each. All these were lively
and ever-present reminders of what might be looked
for by any demented publisher who paid for the printing of *The Certain Hour*.

Nor did the long and ill-starred career of *The
Certain Hour* fail by-and-by to end with an appro-
priately tragic dénouément. In March 1915 this volume of the Biography was accepted by McBride's;
and they, by-and-by—after using, during the sum-

mer months of 1915, the yet unpublished stories in *Lippincott's* (later *McBride's*) *Magazine,*—brought out *The Certain Hour* as a book in November 1916. The dizain's failure, after its nine years of birth-pangs, was so instant and utter that before Christmas it had joined its fellows (to which had now been added *The Rivet in Grandfather's Neck*) on the "remainder" counter.

I ADD merely that the first printing was from type, which was then taken down. Later, in 1920, when we wished to include this book in the Kalki edition, zinc plates were made frugally from a copy of this first and only printing. It thus followed that I had not ever any chance to revise *The Certain Hour* un-til when, in 1928, this book was rewritten for the Storisende edition. I then leaned toward a rather more deliberate astringency than the actual author of this book appears to have admired in 1916; and in consequence I took out, in the interest of con-cision, almost as much material as I then added to *The Certain Hour* for the sake of "distinction and clarity, of beauty and symmetry, of tenderness and truth and urbanity." —Which does not mean that I attained any one of the seven.

The Cords of Vanity

A GREAT deal has been said already—as here the reader may perhaps assent with unflattering vigorousness—about the gallant attitude. We come now to its final aspect,—which is, most naturally, a depiction of the gallant attitude in the relatively modern life of my own generation. I mean that *The Cords of Vanity* depicts the attempt of Robert Etheridge Townsend, between the years 1884 and 1903 of mankind's salvation, "to accept the pleasures of life leisurely and its inconveniences with a shrug."

Of how old Guivric of Perdigon acquired the body of Gerald Musgrave, and so utilized it as to bring the life of Manuel into the Townsend family, both through the Bulmer and the Musgrave line, you may learn in *Something About Eve*. In *The Cords of Vanity* my protagonist—who remains always, as I must repeat, the life of Manuel—now informs the great-grandson of Gerald Musgrave's body, through transitions which the inquisitive may find duly recorded in *The Lineage of Lichfield*.

CONCERNING *The Cords of Vanity* I find all writing, in the chill glare of public opinion, rather difficult. Yet I start temerariously by stating that, during my final revisions of this volume in 1928 for the Storisende edition, *The Cords of Vanity,* howsoever abundant in disastrously written passages which demanded a vast deal of cobbling up, yet as a whole appeared to me a better book than it ever got the credit for being. And to protest that much is really to claim remarkably little, since *The Cords of Vanity* has not ever been liked by anybody. To say that this is the least popular of my books would be to mislead you: for from the first it has been unpopular to the point of violence. It is a book against which, for no reason ever known to me, the majority of its not over many readers have manifested a sort of personal animus. I do not know why. It is a fact which frankly puzzles me. I still cherish for Mr. Townsend a mild sort of pale liking.

THIS book was begun, so clearly as I can now recollect such far-off happenings, early in 1907: I know it was completed in June 1908. Into its making went a variety of material which had previously been published, in the guise of short stories, by the old *Smart Set.* I mean, that primordial *Smart Set* of 1902 and 1903, as Arthur Grissom had founded it, and as it was then edited by Marvin Dana and Charles Han-

son Towne. Interblended with this material were
one or two brief essays thitherto unprinted . . . The
book was originally written, I can recollect, in the
third person. I believe, in fact, the entire comedy
was completed in this form. Then all was recast in
the first person, with Townsend telling his own tale:
and I have sometimes thought that through this
process *The Cords of Vanity* may, somehow, have
acquired a suggestion of rather unhuman detachment, and of callousness, such as many people profess to find in this book, although I confess that by
me this flavor remains undiscovered.

The typescript was accepted by Doubleday, Page
& Company, who after all had not lost any money on
The Eagle's Shadow, and so had fair hopes for my
second novel. But in 1907, between the filing of
Howard Pyle's protest against illustrating any more
of my work and the publication of *Gallantry* in the
midst of a money panic, my literary luck had turned.
The Eagle's Shadow had approximately paid its own
expenses in 1904, whereas in 1905 its immediate suc-
cessor in point of publication, *The Line of Love*,
had enjoyed a tiny success. Thereafter, until 1920,
every book which I could manage to get published—
with, quite naturally, in my ever-thickening aura of
failure, an always increasing difficulty—was to be a
commercial disaster; and from critical standpoints
was to attract, at best, a few words of condescending
dismissal, or, at worst, of abuse. I report thankfully

that I have never printed anything which did not annoy a reasonable number of persons.

The Cords of Vanity, then, appeared as a book in March 1909, after having been held over from publication in the preceding autumn, through its publishers' vain hope that this story might be found serialisable by one or another magazine. It was published, I repeat: and I discover that a then unfamous H. L. Mencken wrote most politely concerning this novel, in the June 1909 *Smart Set.* It is a fact which shows that Mencken, even thus long ago, was unique, because all other verdicts differed from his verdict quite perceptibly.

"THE nauseating confessions of a cur," was the summing up of the New York *World,* whereas the more kindly *Sun* found the book to be merely "a morass of fatuous philandering." Both, if but tacitly, assumed —as, I must here record, did all my other reviewers, with a rather embarrassing unanimity—that I was in this book rendering an exact history of my own life. The *Times* (also published in New York City) adopted, as was the way of the *Times,* even in 1909, a more moral tone: "Men with red blood in their veins consider the man who brags of his love-affairs an abnormal, contemptible sort of person. This book arouses nausea and a keen desire for fresh air and lemons." The New York *Press,* however, was dis-

pleased upon somewhat different grounds: "We confess to losing interest in the tale early in the second
chapter when Robert Etheridge Townsend describes
his mother as 'the silly, pretty woman.' An author
who thinks readers will become interested in a hero
who will describe his mother in such terms labors
under a queer impression of humanity and its sym-
pathies."

Thus ran the metropolitan verdict upon a book
which the provinces acclaimed with no dissimilar dis-
missals. "The book will come under the general
head of trash," remarked succinctly the Springfield
(Massachusetts) *Republican*; and I have no reason
whatever to believe that New England dissented
with its time-tested spokesman. The opinion of the
Middle-West I take to have been voiced by the
Cleveland (Ohio) *Leader*: "Robert Etheridge
Townsend is contemptible and unclean. He is not the
sort of fellow clean-minded girls and women wish to
read about." And for the Far West spoke the
San Francisco (California) *Argonaut*—concerning,
through that ever-present assumption, not Mr. Townsend, but merely me,—"A commonplace and con-
ceited young man, for some inscrutable reason, feels
impelled to take the world into his confidence on the
subject of his many love-affairs."

The South, of course, did not notice in 1909 that
this or any other work of fiction had been published
since Amélie Rives brought out *The Quick or the*

Dead in 1888,—which, even so, the majority of
Southerners had read, not in book form, but in a
borrowed copy of *Lippincott's Magazine*. And for
the Middle Atlantic States, I find the Utica (New
York) *Observer* to have summed up all essentials
quite nicely, and to have rounded off the national
verdict,—"It has never been considered good taste
to relate such experiences in public, much less to
write them out in a book."

In brief—nobody dissenting except that unknown
H. L. Mencken,—*The Cords of Vanity* was dismissed to limbo, and was "remaindered" with rather
bewildering swiftness. That was the end of it until
in 1920 this book was republished in the Kalki edition . . . . I regret that I have not space here to
record the printed tributes which this tale evoked in
this second avatar. These later tributes lacked the
sturdy moral flavor of 1909; but in warm friendli-
ness, I can assure you, they were equally deficient.
The book proved in 1920, and it remains to this date,
I can but repeat, unpopular to the point of violence.
And, as I began by saying, I quite honestly do not
know why.

WHEN in 1928 I set about rewriting this book for
the Storisende edition, I found, in rummaging among
my old manuscripts, that the young man who first
wrote this book had begun, and had partially fin-

ished, an Author's Note for *The Cords of Vanity*,
written in, to all appearance, 1908. It is headed "Suppressed Foreword for *The Cords of Vanity: rough
draft.*" Well, and a rough draft not ever completed,
it very plainly is. I had forgotten about this Foreword: and I do not in the least recollect why it was
not ever polished off by its writer and used with the
book. Yet I debate, too, if it was ever meant to be
printed? for, despite its heading, it has much the air
of those now rather pathetic notes, as to his literary
plans and his half-formed notions, which the young
fellow so often wrote to himself for his own special
benefit.

I quote, in any event, from this ancient fragment,
a paragraph or two which seem to me yet valid:

"Then, too, the book is disproportionate throughout. Scenes where Mr. Townsend holds the stage's
centre are elaborated; scenes wherein he plays—not
quite a sorrier, but, rather a less important part—are
scamped remorselessly. The characters of other people are very vaguely indicated; for only in his own
peculiarities and inconsistencies does he find a spectacle of unfailing interest. So, he is naïvely astounded
when he discovers that Stella has certain personal
characteristics, after all. For the man, at bottom,
looked upon other people as adjuncts, as being created, with trees and butterflies and the sidereal hosts
of space, to diversify the world he lived in and pre-
vent its being to him monotonous.

"From the first he is avoiding anything unpleasant, asking aid in his attempt from God and the devil
impartially. Mr. Townsend to every appearance considered that he deteriorated by gradations: but you
and I, reading, see he did not change at all. And he
is abundant in allusion to his assumed childishness;
yet we find him quite seriously maintaining the child's
standard of ethics and rationality to the end.

"Always his egoism blinds him: personally, I esteem it debatable if, from the first, Miss Mont-
morenci was any better than might in reason be expected of her, just as I question whether she blushed
violently enough for him to observe the phenomenon
by moonlight. I find it entirely plausible that, after
all, Mrs. Hardress may have told upon her death-
bed the truth. For the rest, I cannot fathom the relations of Mr. Townsend with Agnés Faroy or Celia
Reindan: I am sure, however, that they are elided
because in these two commerces his self-admiration
somehow came a cropper. Again there is a certain
vagueness touching Mrs. Mounteagle, and, for that
matter, as concerns the Comtesse d'Arlanges.

"But I believe the man was writing the truth as
he saw or seemed to remember it, and so I have let
that which was written stand unaltered; and, for one,
I find what he omitted [is] as characteristic as much
that he recorded . . .

"In a phrase, I take this book to be a picaresque
romance of hedonism, and have so labelled it. Or—

to employ another figure—his egoism always is as
a thick mist about this Robert Etheridge Townsend.
As concerns other persons the mist distorts and even
blinds his vision: but as concerns himself, it forms a
tent wherein he feels at liberty to strut before his
mirror Adam-naked."

WELL, that is rather vilely phrased, here and there,
of course. The final metaphor appears peculiarly unhappy; and manages but to suggest that Townsend,
naked before his mirror, in such a remarkably heavy
mist, incurs large danger of pneumonia. Nor do I
whole-heartedly admire "the sidereal hosts of space"
when they invade a communication thus casual. The
quotation shows, though, that during the completing
of this book Stella's sister was elevated in rank and
became a marquise in good time for publication—
although Lizzie's original, I may here mention,
adorns the peerage of a country other than France.
It shows that at one season or another *The Cords of
Vanity* was subtitled A Picaresque Romance of
Hedonism. It shows, I obscurely feel in regarding
that mention of Mrs. Hardress, some later change in
the author's first plan concerning her. And it shows,
to me at least, one or two of the aims of this book's
young writer which he did not altogether attain.
     But in the main point of every creative writer's
business he did, I think, succeed. He created, that is,

a character which has some actual vitality. Townsend
appeared to me, during my final revisions of this
book in 1928, rather real. I have found, to be sure,
that my present-day opinion of Townsend as a person is not quite the self-evident opinion of the young
man who first wrote about Townsend. I think, for
example, that the deviser of Townsend worked rather
more subtly than he knew, in that Townsend does
change during the book's progress. And I detect in
Townsend somewhat less of depravity and more of
foolishness than his youthful creator, I suspect, ever
intended to exist. But the point is that I can agree
with my young namesake, and, for that matter, with
all the most unfriendly critics of Robert Etheridge
Townsend, in considering Townsend as one considers
an actual human being. The point is that, to my so
much older and perhaps age-damaged eyes, Townsend seems rather real. There the defence rests.

In any case, it has appeared well to lend to my
commentary a flavor of the authoritative by quoting
thus extensively from the actual author of *The Cords
of Vanity*. His random jottings have afforded—
again, to me at least—some first-hand information
as to what in point of fact the young fellow was
about. So I have esteemed these ancient and awkwardly worded paragraphs to be the book's most fit
introduction to the world's unhappily non-existent
attention.

They remain valid, I believe, in every respect which

occurs to me, except that in the Storisende version of this book, among divers other changes, Miss Mont- morenci blushes less violently. But no reader of my Comedy of Shirking, I am certain, will blush at all, inasmuch as a great deal more than any passage of time divides us nowadays from that remote year of grace 1909, when even *The Cords of Vanity* also was a nauseatingly unclean book offensive to the good taste of American journalism.

From the Hidden Way

THIS seems to me, in some sort, a volume of parentheses. Yet I think that Mr. Townsend's verse is a quite essential part of his portrait and of his gallant trifling with just half serious emotions, in an age not favorable to a leisurely acceptance of life's pleasures, or of its pains either. For that reason I have collected his verses—to which divers references have been made in *The Cords of Vanity*, and from which several extracts, whether with or without due acknowledgment, have been cited elsewhere in the Biography—and I have printed these verses in *From the Hidden Way*.

I do not accord them the courtesy title of poems. It is all, as for that matter most masculine verse ought to be, the verse of a very young man. And it appears to me to round off the portrait of Townsend by evoking, after the completion of *The Cords of Vanity*, a figure not unfamiliar to anybody who has read the Biography thus far. I mean, the boy that one used to be and is not any longer . . . During my revisions of the Biography for the Storisende edition

I found that boy ubiquitous. He enters the seventh
chapter of *Beyond Life*. He is the crux of the earliest
written short story, Love-Letters of Falstaff, and he
confronts Gerald Musgrave at the end of the lateliest written of all the comedies. Equally does the
opening tale of the completed Biography end with
Manuel's discovery of that boy in the pool of Haran-
ton, just as you may find the Biography itself to end
with the coming of the author of *The Eagle's Shadow*
into the library of the author of *Jurgen*. The intervening appearances of this boy are to be listed in
large numbers rather than in the space here at my
disposal. It is enough to say that virtually all the inheritors of Dom Manuel's life have encountered this
boy at one or another turn of their fortunes . . .
Well, in *From the Hidden Way* alone does this
omnipresent stripling speak directly to you at any
length: and logic urges that the person who enters
the Biography more often than any other person is
entitled to at least the major part of one volume all
to himself.

THAT boy I have found everywhere in my writings,
I repeat, just as I have found everywhere a variant
of one "situation." I mean, the encounter of two persons between whom love has existed, and who speak
together, as they believe, for the last occasion in
their lives.

If I do not at once tell you the exact number of times that this "situation" occurs in the Biography, it is simply because, after I had found it some sixty times, I stopped counting. But all through the Biography I have discovered the refrain: "You have been to me the most important person in the world. I shall not ever see you again. So now let us speak truthfully." And side by side with this I have found another refrain: "I am that which you were, and are not any longer. You will not ever see me again. So now let us speak truthfully."

Just why these two special notions should have thus haunted me throughout all of twenty-five years I do not know. But I do know that in my writings they are apparent everywhere. So I suppose I must believe, at the bottom of my heart, that if ever any man were for one instant to be candid with the person most nearly intimate with him, or were to be candid with himself, it would be an unparalleled and a highly interesting adventure.

—All which is but a prologue to the statement that, although these verses may seem remarkably alien from their graying author, whom I to-day meet but rarely in Lichfield, in his staid and honored middle life, yet I suspect them to be an integral part of him even now. So I include these verses in the Biography as a portion of his portrait, and as an appendix, which but for its forbidding length would have been a parenthesis, to *The Cords of Vanity.*

THE verses in *From the Hidden Way* date mainly, in their first forms, from 1895 to 1900. So near as I can recall, The Castle of Content is the most ancient of these metrical indiscretions. I know it was written either in the October or the November of 1895; and I find this lament for so long evanished youth to be a characteristic production for a boy of sixteen. But all these verses were revised, and were yet again revised, until as late as 1912. In the spring of that year they were put into very much their final form. The changes which have been made since then, while omnipresent, and the rhymes of a less ancient date in composition, are few.

From the Hidden Way was produced in book form —through one of those shrugged concessions with which publishers now and then humor the childishness of authors—in the November of 1916. We did not expect the volume to pay for the expense involved in printing it; and its success as a marketable product did not in anything betray our expectations. I was to receive a royalty, my publishers agreed, "for all copies of said Work actually sold by them, after 750 copies have been sold." But as they printed only 620 copies, I rather fancy that clause was meant from the first to be sarcastic.

The book was republished in the Kalki edition, in 1924: and the receipt of my royalty statements as to *From the Hidden Way* has remained since then a semi-annual humiliation.

THEN again, in August 1928, the Crosby Gaige Company published, in a limited edition, *Ballades from the Hidden Way,* with the following self-explanatory preface. I quote this preface because its tenor is by no means restricted to the ballades.

"Hereinafter I have but somewhat re-arranged those verses in ballade form which compose a part of *From the Hidden Way.* They are perhaps not the least faulty of the rhymes to be found in a scrap-heap which contains nowhere, to my twentieth century taste, anything absolutely earth-staggering in merit. But the boy who wrote them left at his decease, as it happens, just enough ballades—or, in any event, just enough verses which were virtually ballades—to make up a volume of the exact size desired by my present publishers. It was an accident which appeared so plainly providential that I have preferred to shift responsibility; and to let coincidence serve as the real editor in the shaping of this selection.

"Now that it is made I weigh the result with very liberally miscellaneous emotions. Yet, after all, Landor has here said the last word:—'I would not stand upon my verses: it is a perilous boy's trick, which we ought to leave off when we put on square shoes. Let our prose show what we are, and our poetry what we have been.'

"I permit this volume, then, to serve its purely Landorian end. And I have dedicated it, perforce, to the lady whom for the longest period of time I have regarded with a respectful and quite hopeless affection."

The lady referred to was Mrs. Millamant: and the dedicatory verses are nowadays to be found in the Storisende text of *From the Hidden Way* under the title "The Way of the World."

From the Hidden Way has thus come, in its final form, to contain with some philanthropic exceptions nearly all the verse I have ever printed. I have included all rhymes which seemed to me—almost—able to stand alone, through howsoever minor merits, as individual productions.

I have omitted some of the verses contributed, during 1895-98, to the *William and Mary College Monthly*: none of them, by excellent luck, were signed with my name, and nobody can ever prove that I wrote them. I have included only one of the *Sonnets from Antan*, because, whensoever these sonnets are regarded in disjunction from the explanatory notes which Gerald Musgrave made for them, they appear, to me at least, rather meaningless. The other *Sonnets from Antan*, along with their notes, may be found in the last volume of the Storisende edition.

I have left out, through similar reasons, the acrostic dedications to *Beyond Life, The Silver Stallion* and *Jurgen*, as well as the heroically rhymed

Prologue and Epilogue to *Gallantry*. I have omitted, too, the sirvente which young Duke Jurgen composed in honor of the Princess Guenevere, if only because to include his outcry would be to take a side in the as yet unsettled question, whether or no this sirvente be truly a sonnet? Bülg's testimony here, as in so many other places, seems inconclusive. And I have included only one of my experiments in contrapuntal prose, taking this from *Something About Eve*, after some brief hesitation over a few other essays in this kind of which the forms are more strictly metrical, such as Manuel's explanation of the figure he desires to make, in the seventh chapter of *Figures of Earth*, and Miramon Lluagor's not unremarkable outburst of hexameters in the fourth chapter, as well as the inscription which Jurgen found upon the sign-board in the fifth chapter of his adventurings.

I PAUSED rather longer in considering *Big Names and Little Verses*. This, one should here explain, was a mildly regrettable volume published in 1915, to which a vast and very mixed lot of writers and illustrators contributed; and of which the proceeds, such as they were, went to a philanthropic organization which aimed to purvey a dependable brand of milk to indigent babies. Across the many years since 1915 I can just cloudily recall being asked to write a set of verses for this pot-pourri. But one finds therein, instead, signed with my name, only an apologetic and disclamatory note to the lady editors. It is here quoted in full:

"Mesdames,—Your compilation is a book I would have taken pride to figure in if it had not unfortunately been beyond my powers, or by hook or crook, to write in verse—or, rather, what might look like verse if printed so as to begin each line with capitals.

"I hate like sin to have to say so, but you much mistook my capabilities—and flattered me thereby, of course—in thinking that I would have skill to fashion verses fit to be identified with any cause so good as your most meritorious charity, which I would gladly further if I could."

That note, I am told, is incidentally a sonnet. But for one reason and another I preferred not to take advantage of the coincidence; and in consequence this note was not included in *From the Hidden Way.*

WITH then these dubious and few exceptions, you may find in *From the Hidden Way* all the verses which I have ever printed. In preparing the Storisende edition of this book I once more re-arranged these verses with a becoming punctiliousness: for I cannot but regard them with the respect appropriate to their not inconsiderable age, when I reflect that virtually all these rhymes date from another century. These samples of late Victorian verse have been prinked and

titivated continually since they first came into being:
indeed, in the Storisende version I made yet again
some improving changes from the earlier version of
the Kalki edition: but, upon the whole, these verses,
howsoever often revised, yet remain to-day very
much as they were originally written, during the last
years of the nineteenth century. This is one of the
few volumes which in the Storisende edition of my
books I did not rewrite utterly.

One touches here the annoying defect of all verse.
Prose, which aspires toward loftier goals, is, as Stev-
enson has phrased it, "never done": for an actually
good prose style aims well beyond that which is
possible to human achievement, and so incurs no
danger of perfection. In consequence, you can always
and forever tinker with any imaginable prose passage
and improve it, if only by just a little. Verse, though,
in its perpetually young fields, and within its more
sharp limitations, is but too apt by-and-by to become
perfect, through ever-faithful revision. It becomes
perfect in that it has been made, whether really good
or no, at any rate everywhere as good as it ever can
be made. For that reason (even over and above the
glowing narrow-mindedness, the obsession by some
but partial truth, which good verse demands) no
mentally adventurous and no mature writer can be
interested very long or very gravely by verse-making.
Verse finally gets finished as completely as a cross-
word puzzle.

These verses have, in my opinion, reached that state. —Which is but another way of saying that, although not for one illusory instant can I think they are remarkably fine verses, I do incline to hope that, after some-and-thirty years of repolishment, they are about as good as my personal bardic talents could ever make them.

The Jewel Merchants

WITH *The Jewel Merchants* the Biography concludes its consideration of the gallant attitude toward life. In this my sole attempt at play-writing has the code of gallantry been carried to its utmost possible extreme, in that here alone in the Biography is this code presented unshackled, in a milieu wholly unmoral. *The Jewel Merchants* thus presents gallantry *in excelsis*, or—if you so prefer—*in profundis*. You may find, by the bye (should you indeed be so ill-advised as to waste any time in making this comparison), that by rather long odds such is not the case with the short story upon which *The Jewel Merchants* is founded.

For these reasons, to my best judgment, must *The Jewel Merchants* be ranked separately as an individual unit among the twenty units of the Biography: and yet too, to my auctorial prejudices and to my pricked conscience as a prosateur, does this playlet at times seem to be disposed of far preferably as an accidental excrescence from the Biography, as a sort of uncaptivating wart. I refer to those depressing occasions upon which I consider *The Jewel Merchants* as reading-matter.

SO DOES prudence here urge me to forestall detection, by conceding that this brief play has not any pretensions to "literary" merit. It is a piece in its inception designed for, and in its making swayed by, the requirements of the Little Theatre stage. The one virtue which anybody anywhere could claim for *The Jewel Merchants* as a work of art is the fact that it "acts" easily and rather effectively.

Candor compels the admission forthwith that the presence of this anchoritic merit in the wilderness is hardly due to me. When just after the Christmas of 1920 untoward circumstances and my pliant disposition and the Little Theatre League of Richmond all combined to bully me into promising to the last-named a dramatization of the short story called Balthazar's Daughter, as it appears in *The Certain Hour*, then I docilely converted this tale into a one-act play of which you will find in *The Jewel Merchants* hardly a half-dozen sentences. The comedy I wrote upon this occasion is now at one with the lost dramaturgy of Pollio and of Posidippus; and is even less likely ever to be resurrected for mortal auditors.

It "read," I still think, well enough. I am certain that, when it came to rehearsal, the thing did not "act" at all; and that its dialogue, whatsoever its rhetorical graces, had the defect of being unspeakable. So, at each further rehearsal, we—by which inclusive pronoun I would embrace the actors and the production staff at large, and with especial (metaphorical) ardor Miss Louise Burleigh, who directed all—we, I repeat, changed here a little, and there a little more. We shifted this bit; we deleted another bit; and we "tried out" everybody's suggestions generally, until we at least got the relief of witnessing at each rehearsal a different play. And steadily my first typescript was enriched with interlineations, to and beyond the verge of legibility, as steadily I substituted, for the speeches I had rewritten yesterday, the speeches which the actor (having perfectly in mind the gist but not the phrasing of what was meant) had to-day delivered naturally.

This process did not further any æsthetic splendors. But it did make for what we particularly wanted, which was a play that the League could stage for half an evening's entertainment along with *The Florist Shop*. This process left existent not a shred of the rhetorical fripperies which I had concocted unaided, making of the first public performance of *The Jewel Merchants*, in the February of 1921, a collaboration with almost as many contributing authors as though the production had been a musical comedy.

Well, and I like to think that if only fate had gifted me with an exigent conscience and a turn for

oratory, I would have publicly confessed, at that first
public performance, to all those tributary clarifying
common-sense aids to the play's progress. As it was,
vainglory combined with an aversion to "speech-
making" so immorally as to beget a smirking acceptance of the curtain-call with which an indulgent
audience flustered the nominal author of *The Jewel
Merchants.* My conscience still troubles me about
that curtain-call. Here it is due my collaborators
to tell you that *The Jewel Merchants*, in the outcome,
amply fulfilled the shared purpose of its makers, by
being enacted to a polite amount of applause,—and
it is a pleasure to add that this *succes d'éstime* was
in very little chargeable to anything which I contributed to the play.

FOR another matter, I would here confess that *The
Jewel Merchants*, in addition to its "literary" deficiencies, lacks moral fervor. It will, I trust, corrupt
no reader irretrievably, to untraversable leagues beyond the last hope of redemption; even so, it is a
frankly unethical performance. You must accept this
resuscitated trio, if at all, very much as they actually
went about Tuscany, in long ago discarded young
flesh, when a luxury everywhere common to their
milieu was the absence of any moral excitement over
such-and-such an action's being or not being "wicked."
Now this phenomenon of Renaissance life, as lived

in Italy in particular, has been discussed, time and again, by a vast number of persons. I lack here the space, and the desire, and for that matter, the scholarship, either to explain or to apologize for the era's delinquencies. I would merely indicate that this point of conduct is the fulcrum of *The Jewel Merchants*.

The play presents three persons, to any one of whom the committing of murder or theft or adultery, or any other such-like divinely interdicted feat, is just the risking of the penalty provided against the breaking of that special law if you have the vile luck to be caught at it. This to the people of *The Jewel Merchants* is all that "wickedness" can mean. We nowadays are encouraged, both by the clergy and the police force, to think differently: but such dear privileges do not entitle us to ignore the truth that had any one of the three characters of *The Jewel Merchants* at all honored our present-day standards of behavior, it would have been in radical irreverence of the best-thought-of tenets of the best people. To the cultured there was no generally recognized criminality in crime, but only a perceptible risk. So must this trio adhere gallantly to the accepted customs of their era, and regard an infraction of the Decalogue (for an instance) very much as we but the other day looked on a violation of our Prohibition laws.

In fact, the status which we accorded the Eighteenth Amendment to the Constitution of the United

States prior to its repeal was at this time the status reserved for the Catholic faith and for ethics in general. You found yourself confronted by occasionally enforced, if obviously unreasonable, supernal statutory decrees, which everybody disobeyed now and then as a matter of course. Every now and then, somebody was caught in this disobedience, and the offender was punished, either in this world or the next, without his ill-fortune's involving any disgrace or particular reprehension. As has been finely said, righteousness and sinfulness were for the while "in strange and dreadful peace with each other. The wicked man did not dislike virtue, nor the good man vice: the villain could admire a saint, and the saint could excuse a villain, in things which we often shrink from repeating, and sometimes recoil from believing."

Such was the sixteenth-century Tuscan view of "wickedness" and of "goodness." I have endeavored to reproduce this extreme development of the gallant code without adding to my reproduction the impertinence of criticism from any modern standpoint.

SO MUCH of ink and paper and typography may be needed, I fear, to remind you, in a more exhortatory civilization, that Graciosa is really, by all the standards of her day, a well-reared and well-behaved young woman. To the prostitution of her body, whether with or without the assistance of an ecclesiastically acquired bed-fellow, she looks forward as unconcernedly as you must by ordinary glance out of your front window, to face a vista so familiar that the discovery of any change therein would be troubling. Meanwhile she wishes this sorrow-bringing Eglamore assassinated, as the obvious, the most convenient, and indeed the only way of getting rid of him: and toward the end of the play, alike for her and Guido, the presence of a corpse in her garden is merely an inconvenience without any touch of the gruesome. Precautions, of course, must be taken to meet the emergency, for to be saddled with the corpse of a potentate is awkward; but in the dead body of a man, whom between them they happen to have killed, the lovers can detect nothing more appalling, or more to be shrunk from, than would be apparent if the lifeless object in the walkway were a dead flower. The thing ought to be removed, if only in the interest of tidiness; but there is no call to make a pother over it.

As for our Guido, he is best kept conformable to modern tastes, I suspect, by nobody's prying too closely into the earlier relations between the Duke and his handsome minion. The insistently curious may resort to history to learn at what price the favors of Duke Alessandro were secured and retained: it is no part of the play.

Above all, though, I must remind you that the Duke is unspurred by malevolence. A twinge of jealousy there may be, just at first, to find his pampered Eglamore so far advanced in the good graces of this pretty girl, but that is hardly important. Thereafter the Duke is breaking no law, for the large reason that his preference in any matter is the only law thus far divulged to him. As concerns the man and the girl he discovers on this hill-top, they, in common with all else in Tuscany, are the possessions of Duke Alessandro. Reflection can raise no question as to how he "ought" to deal with them, for to your chattels, whether they be your finger rings or your subjects or your fine palaces or the fair quires of paper upon which you indite your verses, you cannot rationally be said to "owe" anything. No, the Duke is but a spirited lad in quest of amusement: and Guido and Graciosa are the playthings with which, on this splendid sunlit morning, he attempts to divert himself.

All three of the play's characters, in brief, during the some forty minutes of the play's action behave in consonance with the gallant code, in—as I began by saying—a milieu wholly unmoral; and the thwarted ideals of Robert Etheridge Townsend, which could find in Lichfield no outlet, take form handsomely, in the garden of Balthazar Valori, as Duke Alessandro de Medici.

The Jewel Merchants was first performed by the Little Theatre League of Richmond, Virginia, on 22 February 1921. The play appeared in the *Smart Set* magazine, July 1921; and was published in book form, December 1921, in an edition limited to 365 copies. It then had among the Little Theatre companies of America its small vogue, being presented by some thirty of them upon various occasions; and in fact as lately as 1934 *The Jewel Merchants* was being most captivatingly rendered, by a superb troupe of marionettes, in Dalton, Georgia. It has also been made the basis of an opera which, I regret to report, still lacks a producer because of America's unwillingness to encourage American composers.

I need add only that in due course *The Jewel Merchants* was somewhat revised—though I did not dare much to meddle with a text which experience had proved to be the best practical text,—and this play was included in the Storisende edition of the Biography, in 1929.

The Rivet in Grandfather's Neck

AS IN *The Cords of Vanity* one has dealt with the gallant attitude in modern conditions, so now this volume of the Biography considers Colonel Rudolph Musgrave's life-long pursuit of chivalrous ideals in very much the same era and circumstances. Of the Musgrave family you may have heard previously, either in *The Line of Love* or in *Something About Eve*; and R. V. Musgrave's history of the clan has been cited more than once. We pass now to the history of the historian himself.

In this book the life of Manuel, when it is viewed lineally, informs—to be in this place as precise as our chosen genealogist would himself have chosen to be —the body of Rudolph Vartrey[21] Musgrave (1856-1927), who was grandson to Gerald Musgrave's brother, Theodorick Quentin[19] Musgrave II (1780-1850). Viewed subjectively, the life of Manuel here makes its last recorded attempt at a maintenance of the chivalrous attitude toward human existence; and does not manage matters over-happily in its fond adherence to the code of what I have seen

alluded to, in one or another connection, as Southern chivalry.

The code of Southern chivalry has been discussed
by so many gifted pens that we more prosaic persons
who use typewriters tend to avoid the theme. But
above all, this code has been discussed by many
voices, by practised and sonorous voices emanating
from that lofty and, to every appearance, that slightly
tipsifying atmosphere which is breathed by me-
ridional orators upon platforms. Happily, therefore,
here is no need for me to discuss this code. I have
recorded how Gerald Musgrave attempted to escape
its jurisdiction. I now present, in Rudolph Musgrave,
an honest servitor of this code,—within the field of
his own innate limitations.

I TAKE it that Rudolph Musgrave fulfilled the main
requirements of chivalry. He served his geas, in so
far that he frankly accepted, in theory at least, every
obligation which life laid upon him. But he, almost as
frankly, preferred to the performance of a mere drab
obligation the executing of a fine gesture which he
himself could cordially admire. He was, in short, a
gentleman: and I am tempted here to define a gentleman as an insane creature who aspires to make his
pride in his ancestors mutual.

Moreover, Rudolph Musgrave had never any
least doubt that he went about this world as his

Heavenly Father's representative in a place which
was not Rudolph Musgrave's real home. Yet, here.
also, the Colonel was not in everything a second
Edward Longshanks or another Adhelmar de Puysange. The Colonel desired to stay away from that
supernal home as long as might be humanly possible;
he preferred, upon the whole, not ever to think about
that home: and his own well-meant actions during
that unavoidable journeying homeward appeared to
him, for a self-conceded child of God, a bit awkwardly inadequate. The poor man did, in brief, his
utmost: but, as my title-page will forewarn you, this
is a Comedy of Limitations.

Then, as concerns the woman-worship phase of
chivalry, you may note that to this Rudolph Musgrave Anne Willoughby remained his chosen lady in
domnei for a long while. She stayed to him, in a way
with which his wife was in no wise concerned, the
living, the signal and the unflawed symbol of all divine loveliness and of superhuman perfection.
Throughout some thirty-five years of his life he thus
remained Anne Willoughby's adoring and despairing
servitor, at a convenient distance, until a plaguy
chance removed any further need of that despair
with which his adoration was blended inseparably.
For now, of all calamities, his lady in domnei was
preparing to marry him. It really was (in his own
figure) a bit too much like being proffered ice-cream
soda for breakfast during the remainder of one's

life-time. In a situation so unspeakably dreadful, for any true romantic, one must counterfeit, of course, an exterior of joy: but none the less there was nothing for it save to escape—precisely as, when an estray and vitally bankrupt Gerald faced the swine of Horvendile, Gerald Musgrave had escaped—in a cloud of comforting and bravely colored words. There was nothing for it but yet another very fine gesture, which would evade defeat, after all, by refusing to acknowledge the existence of defeat. I am not sure that such was a tender-hearted old Harrowby's explanation of the fifty-seventh chapter; being himself a thorough-paced romantic, he could bear only to glance at this notion, almost bashfully, as a possible contributing cause: but, I admit, it is my explanation.

For words were, to both of these Musgraves, alike an anodyne and a fetish. So the comedy of Rudolph Musgrave's life begins with his hair-breadth escape from the all-destroying printed word; and it bids fair to end with those highly oratorical, post-prandial-sort-of words which serve as a narcotic to ease him out of human living, when at the end of that well-bred entertainment which has been his life he touches, yet again, upon the unparalleled renaissance of the New South which all Southern after-dinner speakers have known to be immediately immanent for the last fifty years. Yet I would have you note that the comedy does not end thus. At the very last, through this cloud

of words which had befogged the man's whole living,
comes the one thing which was real.

YOU may recall what Queen Freydis has said about
the power of words,—"There is give and take, of
course, but, in the main, man is more subservient to
words than they to him." So here, to my finding, the
dangerous stark tyranny of words is the evil principle of *The Rivet in Grandfather's Neck*. The
book is a comedy of limitations; it is a comedy of
neo-chivalry; but it is also a comedy of words which
serve as fetishes, as anodynes, and as intoxicants, in
the while that reality is resolutely not faced.

Of Lichfield's thaumaturgy in the use of words
you may have seen somewhat, in those nine fatal
words, "Evelyn and Gerald have always been such
good friends," against which Gerald Musgrave
strove publicly in vain, just as in private he could do
nothing against those yet more dreadful words: "I
trusted you. I gave you all." In *The Rivet in Grandfather's Neck* you may note yet other instances of
yet other words' work in this same Lichfield: such
as those smug words with which Rudolph Musgrave
ignored the known cause of his sister's malady, even
in his own most private dealings with her; such as
those over-efflorescent words which the man wrote
impartially to Aline Van Orden and to Clarice Pen-
domer and to Patricia Stapylton, and to how many

other pleased fair correspondents, in a sort of auto-intoxication born of his own bubbling rhetoric; and such words, too, as those flamboyant formulas which, whensoever he arose to address a select company in well-bred surroundings, nourished the self-compla-cency of Lichfield and kept Rudolph Musgrave an unfailing social success. This story is, in brief, about the adventuring of a genuine, deep, and wholly hon-est chivalry, as it deals with words; with words which ignore that reality whose place they have usurped; with words that are deadly once they are printed in the newspapers; with words that are deadly because left unspoken; and, above all, with words that are deadly because they induce self-satisfaction.

It is a much trammeled adventuring in which chiv-alry does not triumph. But, to the other side, it is an adventuring from which Rudolph Musgrave comes not utterly defeated.

FOR the rest, this is the first of the three volumes which I have edited and seen through the press for my now deceased friend, Richard Fentnor Harrowby. I have done my utmost by them, in the way of as-tringent revision, but I admit that their writer's dic-tion and discursiveness and constructive methods have very often baffled me. His wholly dreadful habit of popping, if but occasionally, into the minds of first one and then another of his characters, quite as naïvely as ever did old Nicolas de Caen—or, for that matter, as ever did a majority of the world's leading authors—has in particular bothered his editor, for reasons which are discussed in *Straws and Prayer-Books*. It is my doom, as a writer, to deplore this habit: meanwhile, the deplored habits of Harrowby being the applauded methods of our best literature, it appeared my duty as an editor merely to edit these books.

THIS book was outlined in 1910, and presently was put aside in order that I might begin on *Domnei*. Then *Domnei* in its turn was shelved, in a partially completed state, so that I might return to working upon *The Rivet in Grandfather's Neck*. This Comedy of Limitations was finished in the spring of 1911, in approximately but not quite the shape it now has: and, under a variety of titles, it was rejected during the next year and a half by all the publishers of whom I had ever heard.

In the fall of 1912 *The Rivet in Grandfather's Neck* was given its final title, and was retouched, too, here and there, into what I then thought to be its final form. I now do not remember just what changes were incorporated, but I know that they were all prompted by a proud and high design; for they aimed to make this book a resistless entrant in the Reilly & Britton contest, closed in 1913, which had offered

$10,000 as a prize for the best novel submitted to these publishers in 1912.

During the first months of 1913 I spent this $10,000 many times in imagination. But I had never in such competitions any success. How The Rhyme to Porringer was outclassed by twelve other stories in the *Collier's* 1905 contest, has been recorded in my commentary upon *Gallantry*. Then, as far back as 1899, I played my inglorious part in the Century Company's prize contests—for the best essay and for the best poem severally submitted by a college graduate of 1898,—my ill-starred entrants being that essay on The Comedies of William Congreve which was later used in *Beyond Life*, and the verses Amaimon Visits the Thebaid. Neither of them won even the slight meed of an honorable mention.

Since then reflection has united with experience to console my vanity. I myself since then have served as a judge in a number of such contests; and I have thus reached, through much wonderment and tedium, a suspicion that the great mass of trash and incompetence through which in every prize contest the judges have to labor may perhaps always unfit them to reach any rational decision. I rather think it must temporarily impair the minds of the judges; and I most certainly can think of no reason why it should not.

In any case, when the Reilly & Britton award was made public, the prize had gone to Miss Leona Dalrymple, for her romance entitled *Diane of the Green Van*. Meanwhile my typescript had been returned to me long since: and I was again sending it, in its revised form, from one publisher's office to another.

I HAVE not any notion how many firms in all rejected this book during the four years that it went a-begging in editorial waste-baskets. I find that I have kept only thirteen of the letters which heralded the typescript's return to me, via express: but thirteen was not anywhere near the far more impressive total number of publishers who declined to touch, upon any terms, *The Rivet in Grandfather's Neck*.

The book seems during its wandering to have found only one friend. Hewitt Hanson Howland, then literary adviser to the Bobbs-Merrill Company, labored through some two months, I discover, to induce his firm to accept this book; and I yet have the more than polite letter which commemorated the defeat of his persuasiveness. Such was the minority report, where all the other letters which I have preserved appear remarkably unanimous.

The first of them objects: "The theme of the story is unpleasant. Perhaps we might better say it is repellent: and the plot depends upon a condition of affairs which presents but little human appeal, while some of the details are unpleasant." The second letter states, with the precision of an echo, "The impression left by the story is unpleasant, and we are sure the public would not like it." A third letter, after regretting that the story is "unpleasant," continues a bit more definitely: "The book is not a success. You have not enough plot, enough hold-over interest, to make it a really interesting story. I think also that your climax is disappointing. I distinctly had the feeling at the end that I had somehow missed the point,—that you must have had some reason for writing this story, that I had not grasped" . . . When one comes to think of it, and has properly stressed the word "some," that politely puzzled "You must have had *some* reason for writing this story," was really rather annihilating . . . But a fourth letter rids me of the need of any further quotation, by putting all compactly, "This unpleasant story is not of the sort to suit the popular taste, which we are trying to please."

The trouble—the main trouble, at least—was that women in those days were not permitted to have a deformed pelvis, or any pelvis at all, in print. That in this time of candor may seem incredible: but, none the less, is it as insanely true as is the fact that just one bit of unwise levity, as to an infallible Pope's making a slip in elementary arithmetic, prompted—or, to speak more strictly, maintained—the attack upon *Jurgen*. So here, it was the book's mention of Patricia's deformed pelvis which ruined all: that was the "unpleasant" feature, as I learned later, the

feature which might hardly, in declining to publish
The Rivet in Grandfather's Neck, might hardly be
alluded to, even thus distantly, without a risking of
editorial decency. Thus nobly ruled etiquette over
literature in 1913.

Since then the obstetrics of the human body have
become more familiar to the midwives of literature.
Publishers believe nowadays, with something of the
fanatic's firmness, that a story can be "pleasant" only
in defiance of "the popular taste," which they are
still trying to please; and that "plots" have been
forever relegated to detective stories. But we managed matters quite otherwise in the more polite and
the less sophisticated years between 1911 and 1915.

NEVERTHELESS, in the April of 1915, after four
years of trying to place this book, I did finally succeed in procuring a publisher for *The Rivet in Grandfather's Neck*, in Robert M. McBride & Company;
and I so founded a twenty-year-long association.
There is thus no great harm done by recording that
the editorial staff of McBride's insisted, for many
weeks, that the book ought to end with the present
fifty-sixth chapter, so as to leave Anne Charteris and
Rudolph Musgrave upon the presumed point of living happily forever after. Concerning this matter I
evinced some obstinacy; and, in the end, I was permitted my own headstrong way.

It would be agreeable to add that when this, the first of my books to be published by McBride's, was issued in the autumn of 1915, the years of foiled struggling were repaid by an instant and tremendous success. But life has not always a fine sense of form. So the book did not "sell": the libraries and the larger department stores recoiled frankly from Patricia's pelvis: the novel received just one favorable review—from A. L. S. Wood, of the Springfield (Massachusetts) *Union*,—but it otherwise attracted no special critical attention: and the unarithmeticable publishers who had rejected *The Rivet in Grandfather's Neck* were now justified in full.

The Eagle's Shadow

WITH gallant and with chivalrous examples (as a main theme) the Biography has done, now that we reach *The Eagle's Shadow*. Only the poetic attitude in its last phase stays yet to be weighed. We turn now to considering this—in Lichfield, in twentieth-century conditions, in just the conditions among which you may previously have encountered a gallant Townsend and a chivalrous Rudolph Musgrave,—now that *The Eagle's Shadow* introduces, as *The Cream of the Jest* finally disposes of, Felix Bulmer Kennaston.

These are the second and third books written by the late Richard Fentnor Harrowby which it has been my rather melancholy duty to edit under the drawbacks already implied in my commentary upon *The Rivet in Grandfather's Neck*. I am therefore requesting you to remember always, in reading the Harrowbian trilogy about Lichfield, that Harrowby, just as much as did Townsend or Nicolas de Caen or Captain Francis Audaine, wrote about matters more or less unknown to me (so that I have no touchstone for his veracity), and that he wrote also from his own point of view, which very often, even in the restricted lighting of the facts as he himself records them, I do not altogether share.

Meanwhile, you may note, upon consultation of *The Lineage of Lichfield*, that Felix Kennaston's line of descent from Dom Manuel, through the Bulmer family, was in all the same as that of Robert Etheridge Townsend, inasmuch as the mothers of the two men were sisters. The familiary link therefore does not demand any repeating in this place.

IT SHOULD however be recorded, in this place, that this first book dealing with Felix Kennaston was not originally intended to be a book about Felix Kennaston. Perhaps it is not quite that, even now. In any case, we approach here yet another instance of the occasional insubordination of an author's characters upon which I have already dwelt. I have told you how Ormskirk became the leading personage in *Gallantry* despite my utmost and prolonged endeavors. So here, in the first planning of *The Eagle's Shadow*, the centre of its tiny stage had been reserved for Miss Hugonin and Mr. William Vartrey Woods, in so far as the young author of *The Eagle's Shadow* aimed at all at depicting human character.

In chief he aimed at, as I remember it, "that atmosphere of holiday detachment from the ordinary

duties and obligations of existence" concerning which
John Charteris has spoken, in *Beyond Life*, while
talking about Congreve. In fact, should you turn to
this passage, you may there read yet another commentary, from another angle, upon *The Eagle's
Shadow*,—inasmuch as you will find there a complete
summing up of the young fellow's goal, in this his
picturing of "people solely in a temporary and irre-
sponsible withdrawal from the everyday business of
life" . . . He did not, you see, know very much
about the everyday business of life; and so, with a
sort of callow wisdom, he was resolved to avoid the
tricky theme in his writing. And in the pleasant haze
of this all-softening atmosphere the leading characters were to have been, I repeat, Miss Hugonin
and the chivalrous Mr. Woods.

But in the process of getting the book written,
befell that which, since it has happened in three volumes of the Biography, can hardly be mere accident.
It happened later during the writing of *Domnei*, in
which Perion was to have been the protagonist, and
yet (without my altering any incident of the tale)
was ousted somehow from his planned, prime importance by Demetrios, and indeed was almost, if not
quite, outranked by Ahasuerus also. Even Ayrart de
Montors became a person more vitally sympathetic
than is Perion de la Fôret, I am told, before *Domnei*
was all set down upon paper. And this thing happened yet again during the writing of *The Rivet in*

Grandfather's Neck, wherein Rudolph Musgrave remains, to be sure, the protagonist, and yet, hardly becomes an acquaintance so near to any reader of the story as does John Charteris in the relatively few lines allotted to him . . . What had happened, as I first perceived when I came back to these three half-forgotten books in the joint capacity of reader and of editor, was that the writer of each one of these books, during the writing of it, had unconsciously shifted the main part of his own interest from a chivalrous character to the nearest male character whose attitude was distinctly not chivalrous.

So here, when *The Eagle's Shadow* was completed, it contained more printed matter relative to Mr. Woods than to Mr. Kennaston: but Kennaston was none the less, to any of those rare spirits who had reached the last page of *The Eagle's Shadow*, the more fondly rendered of the two, and the more easily remembered, I think, after the novel was put aside.

I deduce that always those various persons who have collaborated in the writing of the Biography must have found the chivalrous attitude toward human life, howsoever admirable in itself, to be less sympathetic to each one of them, as a person with his own instinctive likes and dislikings, than was either the gallant or the poetic attitude. I do not consider this fact to be of any particular importance: but I do find noteworthy this fact's so long elusion of my consciousness. And I suspect, too, it is this same fact which has caused even the most chivalrous of the Manuelites, as Nicolas de Caen has pointed out, to be "cankered with an irreligious desire to have the affairs of this mortal world proceeding more equably with frail human reason,—a desire which has caused them to serve the fair code of chivalry and domnei with great difficulty" . . . It also appears to be rather more than a coincidence that the writers of the Biography should have put aside chivalry as a main theme as long ago as in 1912; and did not revert to depicting a chivalrous person, save in such highly questionable instances as Dom Manuel and Donander of Évre, until 1929, when (after discovering this omission) I added *The Way of Ecben.*

ONE has been drawn by these considerations a long way from *The Eagle's Shadow.* One found, then, in this book a tolerably competent rendering of Harrowby's fond notions about Margaret Hugonin, which one might fairly present to any reader upon the generous principles outlined in *A Little More About Eve.* One found a modicum of not really very bad writing, just here and there, of which, as a reader, one could approve mildly before setting to work to improve it as an editor. And one found in Felix Kennaston a germ of reality. The man lived, with howsoever low blood pressure. He did not seem to be disposed of and done with forever, as were all the other characters, when once you had finished reading the book. One cloudily knew that more had happened to this Felix Kennaston than was anywhere recorded in *The Eagle's Shadow*. It was some while before these happenings were revealed to me: but in 1914, eleven years after Felix Kennaston first came into being, I discovered myself to be setting down these happenings, via Harrowby, in *The Cream of the Jest*.

—All through which paragraph, be it remarked, the pronouns are carefully selected. For, in preparing the Storisende edition of the Biography, during 1927-30, I found all the books written prior to *The Cream of the Jest* to have been written by persons who are to me, nowadays, comparative strangers. I edited the entire Biography as I best might. But only in *The Cream of the Jest* and in its temporal successors had I any sense of dealing with my own work.

I EDITED the Biography, I repeat, as I best might: and in the main I was guided, always, by the axiom that it is the duty of an editor merely to edit. Yet the verb "to edit" is, when you think of it, rather generously inclusive. So in the course of my editing of this Storisende edition I felt at liberty to make considerable additions in the way of matter which tended to draw the Biography more closely together as a complete whole; of matter which emphasized the repetitiousness with which every human life follows in general outline the lives of its progenitors; as well as of matter which, at the time of the first appearance of the volumes published prior to 1917, could not, for one reason or another, conveniently be printed.

Otherwise, I tried to meddle with the text of each volume not very much more than seemed necessary in the light of the reflection that, after all, this volume was to appear under my name and with my signature attached. If it were not—not quite—I who had written this or that book, it was in any case I who was publishing the book . . . And to this reflection I was able to give far more weight in preparing the Storisende edition than had been permissible in those earlier revisings of some half-dozen of these comedies for the Kalki edition. In preparing the unsigned Kalki volumes (which, moreover, were to be sold separately) it appeared my plain duty to deal with each book as an individual production; and at utmost to make of the book that which the younger man who actually did write it would have made of this book at the period of its writing, if only at this period he had known a little more about writing. I might, that is, try loyally to fulfil his intentions.

But here the conditions were otherwise. In this Storisende edition, which was to be vended only as a complete whole, I felt for the first time at quite entire liberty to handle, from every standpoint, each book as but a chapter in the long Biography of Dom Manuel's perpetuated life. Inasmuch as I was to sign each of these books, I felt, also, at liberty to try a bit more opulently to satisfy myself with that which I was signing,—and signing only after I had weighed everything by no criterion of the book's original writer, but rather by my own standards in the fore-running shadow of my fiftieth birthday.

IN ANY case, *The Eagle's Shadow* was written in 1903 by the young man whom, if you so elect, you may encounter in *Straws and Prayer-Books*. The first thirteen chapters of the comedy, as it now stands, were done in the May of that year. The story was then put aside, until the author returned to it in November 1903, and during this month completed the book.

The typed manuscript went northward in January 1904, to be rejected forthwith by the first publishers to whom it was offered. *The Eagle's Shadow* was accepted, however, by Doubleday, Page & Company, to whom it was next submitted, in February 1904, and who brought out the book in the October of the same year.

During the intervening summer months the story had appeared as a serial which ran through nine issues of the *Saturday Evening Post*. Even thus early did the Biography figure as an introducer of general corruption: for it was during the publication of this serial that the *Post*, after some preliminary correspondence and strong editorial doubts, first admitted to its columns, upon page 10 of the issue dated 24 September 1904, the word "damn" printed shamelessly in full. The speaker was Miss Hugonin, who thus, if she did not add materially to literature, at least created history. It is true that on the very next page Mr. Jukesbury, in his attempt to utter the same word, was allowed only a chastened two-em dash. But this so prompt relapse into refinement proved unavailing, once the laws of good taste had been violated, and the word "damn" accorded this formal epiphany upon every rural delivery route. There was no longer any concealing from the readers of the *Post* the fact that this word existed: and the monosyllable has, since 1904, appeared with reasonable frequency in America's most characteristic magazine.

The Eagle's Shadow, I repeat, was published as a book in October 1904. It was found a regrettable performance, not, I must hastily add, upon such grounds as would now seem obvious, but through reasons for which I must refer you to the Appendix of the present *Eagle's Shadow*. In brief, there were kindly souls so deeply shocked by the immorality of this book that they wrote to the New York *Times* about it; and the *Times* printed the denunciatory letters. A beginning author is not often aided thus generously. Yet even when thus bleated over, as a dire example of pornography, the book did not "sell" beyond—to be precise—the modest extent of 2871 copies. This almost, if not quite, paid the expenses of the book—which its publishers had advertised rather liberally.

Technically this was my first book, although, as I have elsewhere explained, I think that *The Line of Love* was in reality my first book, in so far as I can feel any of the books published under my name prior to 1917 to have been written by me. *The Eagle's Shadow*, in any event, was the first volume to bear my name upon its cover. It thus paved the way, it led almost of necessity, to all those other books whose backbones were to be similarly stamped during the next quarter of a century. And in consequence, whensoever I consider *The Eagle's Shadow*, it raises rather inevitably the question, into which altruism enters not at all, if this self-imposed, long semi-slavery to the Biography has been, to me, worth while?

It is a question which I have no least intention of answering here. But when I recall (with some mental effort) the boy who wrote this book, and those other more or less various young men who contributed analogically various volumes to the Biography, I perceive that, in a wholly saddening sense, their work has outlived them. I seemed then, in 1927-30, when

I prepared the Storisende edition of my books, to
edit the literary remains of a variety of persons with
whom I was not very deeply acquainted. And I sometimes wondered, in the while that I dealt with their
relics, if these various young men might not have
been happier persons, during their so brief lives, if
they had been employed as stockbrokers or as minis-
ters of the gospel or as lawyers or as insurance agents
or as morticians or as governors of their native states,
or, in fine, if they had followed some generally well-
thought-of and common-sense vocation?

I still wonder about this, now and then, disinterestedly. —Disinterestedly, because I reflect that,
after all, these various young and not-so-young men
all did precisely the one thing which each one of
them most wanted to do. The result faces me, in the
Storisende edition of the Biography; and it is with
complete self-satisfaction that I regard the most am-
bitiously planned literary work which has ever come
out of America.

Need I dwell in this place upon the vast difference
between the making of a plan and the executing of it?
I think not. I am so modest as to believe my readers
will have very little trouble in detecting this difference.

Yet me that does not concern. I stay well satisfied,
not with the Biography (which, like a cross-word
puzzle, matters nothing to me now that it is finished)
but with the twenty-eight years—in themselves, a
reasonably long lifetime—of highly enjoyable hard

work which the Biography has offered. In brief, I wanted—and I am sure I do not know why—to write the Biography; so I did write it, with unfailing pleasure; and I cannot think of any moral grounds upon which an entire lifetime of self-indulgence might hope to escape reprehension.

The Cream of the Jest

W E TURN now to the last of the books by
Richard Fentnor Harrowby, which is *The
Cream of the Jest*. Continuing directly with the
matter of *The Eagle's Shadow*, I must tell you—since
Harrowby has omitted this information—that Kathleen Saumarez and Felix Kennaston were married in
June 1904, to confront, as it seemed, a future of
genteel poverty. But, within four months, the death
of old strange Henry Kennaston, the squire of Al-
cluid, had changed all that gray prospect materially.

I avoid further entrance into affairs with which
the Biography of Manuel's life has no close concern,
and which in any case are amply recorded in J. V. A.
Froser's *Biography of Felix Kennaston*. You may
read therein how the elopement of Kennaston's
parents, in 1867, had begun a feud between the two
families,—a feud which had resulted in Kennaston's
being reared by the Bulmers, without any contact
with his father's kindred,—so that, when Henry
Kennaston was killed, in October 1904, his only surviving nephew acquired a competence from a person

whom Felix Kennaston had not ever known or talked
with, nor even seen from a distance . . . The point
here is that Felix Kennaston in his middle thirties became economically independent and was made free
to devote the rest of his days to whatsoever amuse-
ments he might prefer; and that he then gave over his
life to the grinding thraldom of creative writing.

—WHEREBY, of course, American literature was
enriched with *Men Who Loved Alison.* . . . Of the
actual and eventual worth of this romance I cannot
pretend to be an unprejudiced judge. The tale seems
to me one of those many books which have profited,
very dubiously indeed, by having obtained, in one
way or another, the repute of being "indecent." Such
books tend to endure, but their tenure of survival
is upon depressingly twilit terms. And they make for
a most dolorous deal of dreary time-wasting.

Indeed it is quite dreadful to consider with what
sad and futile perseverance the sloppy and soporific
catalogues of Rabelais, the pale inanities of the
Heptameron, and the unendurably dull botcheries of
Boccaccio—or, for that matter, of Fielding and of
Smollett—have been toiled through by misguided
millions in quest of these authors' rumored obscenity.
Yet it is even more dreadful, for the ears of the
fairly honest, to hear any one of these readers protest, as they all do invariably, that he reads not for

the story's sake but because of the delicate art and the sparkling wit with which the tale is told. Besides, he does get, in the way of indecency, so very little for his trouble.

Well, and just so, I doubt if *Men Who Loved Alison*, in common with a great many other modern masterpieces, does not continue to be read to-day upon somewhat similar grounds. As books go, this volume—which was first published, so nearly as I remember, in 1908—has had a long life; and it is handsomely written, of course, in its own over-ornate and self-conscious and clogged fashion. But I fancy that most of this book's readers are, here again, those immature-minded persons who are content to put up with the diction and the stylistic devices for the sake of the atoning talk about unnatural amours which, howsoever sparsely, here and there adorns and cheers the dogged advance of the pornoscopic reader. I fancy, in fine, that *Men Who Loved Alison* has a great many readers of a class with which, "the author of *Jurgen*" may claim familiarity.

IT IS, though, now that I think of it, with another book that this commentary should be concerned. And my appropriate point is, rather, that with *The Cream of the Jest*, the Biography completes the portrayal, begun in *The Eagle's Shadow*, of Felix Bulmer Kennaston and of his adoption of the poetic attitude toward life, in the very same Lichfield which Robert Etheridge Townsend and Colonel Rudolph Musgrave co-etaneously inhabited, and of Kennaston's ultimate success as an Economist. Hereinafter, then, as I have written in another place, the story of the Biography is rounded off by presenting the poet—the *poietes*, the "maker"—in modern conditions; and by presenting, too, the manner of Felix Kennaston's return into Poictesme,—into that all-accommodating country wherein almost anything is rather more than likely to happen,—so that, through this return, the perpetuated life of Manuel ends its seven hundred years of journeying at the exact point of its outset. The circle is thus made complete, as my last poet annihilates, through quite other means than were employed by my first poet, Madoc, the intervening twenty generations.

That is the main point. Madoc triumphed, you may remember, through the amenities of judicious punctuation. Felix Kennaston made use of somewhat different methods to gain very much the same end. But Kennaston also triumphed. And the protagonist of the Biography—that protagonist being, as I have perhaps already said, the perpetuated life of Manuel —was thus enabled, once more, to do that which seemed expected.

I mean, that the life of Manuel, as that life in *The Cream of the Jest* is embodied in Felix Bulmer Kennaston, returned into its long-lost Poictesme. I mean, that the life of Manuel thus did, in a fashion told of in *The Cream of the Jest*, conform to those ancient prophecies which had been begotten, in some part by Jurgen's essays in the imaginative, but in chief by the fond pride and the proud faith of Dame Niafer. I mean that *The Cream of the Jest* tells about how, yet again, "Manuel, as was his custom, did what Niafer thought best,"—inasmuch as this book records how Niafer at long last had her way with her husband, as became a competent wife, a great while after both Manuel and Niafer were reputedly dead. . . . For I doubt if, in any important sense, either one of my primal lovers was truly dead, or ever will be dead so long as the amenities of marriage endure among humankind. We know that the life of Manuel informed the body of Felix Kennaston. But I am equally certain that Niafer survived in Kathleen Kennaston; and that Niafer continues to survive, wheresoever home-life flourishes, in the ageing body of every really competent wife. There is no thriving household but has its Niafer commanding it unostentatiously.

The Cream of the Jest was some while in the making. In January 1911, I think, was begun the dizain which under stars more favorable would have told about ten of Richard Harrowby's adventurings, for the most part, in the occult: but Saturn very plainly

stood in the ascendant at the scheme's birth; for as
these stories came into being, no one of them, save
only Concerning David Jogram, met with the then
present needs of any discoverable magazine. The
dizain was therefore abandoned; and of the eight
stories finished, some were destroyed, while the
others were utilized here and there variously.

Two of these tales, as they had been written in
the spring of 1911, were combined and rewritten in
1913, with the addition of considerable new matter,
so that before 1914 had well begun to make the
world safe for hypocrisy, these stories had blended
into one continuous and fairly long Comedy of Eva-
sion, called then *In the Flesh*, but a little later rechristened *The Cream of the Jest*. . . . Thus did it
come about that with the opening of 1915 this book
set forth, in typescript, to seek the applause of en-
raptured multitudes.

The first of all its rejectors—acting on behalf of
the George H. Doran Company, in January 1915,
—was a romantic-minded and obviously young male
who wrote me as to this book a wholly charming, if
wholly disapproving, long letter. I still treasure it.
His objections I find to have been, severally, that my
theme lacked sufficient weight to ballast more than a
short story; that the portions relative to the publishing of Kennaston's novel (which turned out, later,
to be uncommonly neat soothsaying) could interest
no one unconnected with the world of book-making;

that *In the Flesh* was not verily "in the flesh," but smelt over-strongly of midnight oil; and that, above all, my book failed to present in its characters a group, or even any one person, who evoked the reader's sympathy and admiration. For, as this hyper-critical romanticist went on to explain—prior to sub-scribing himself "Sincerely yours, Sinclair Lewis,"—the general public simply cannot be induced to buy novels about unattractive and ignoble people, al-though the future author of *Main Street* and *Elmer Gantry* did go so far as to admit that disagreeable characters might be permissible "as villains in naïve literature which is still unashamed of melodrama."

In February the typescript of *In the Flesh* was rejected by the J. B. Lippincott Company. For some now inexplicable reason or another it seems to have been declined by no publishing firm during March.

Then, in April 1915, I paid my first visit to the offices of Robert M. McBride & Company, at that time in Union Square, where yet another thitherto unheard-of young person, who signed himself "Guy Holt," had been interested by the typescript of *In the Flesh* to the highly non-committal extent of wish-ing to see something else by its writer. I, who had four unpublished books, was willing to oblige him. So the visit took place in due form; and thus began, upon my thirty-sixth birthday, the most staunch and the most beneficent of all my literary friendships. Moreover, in the upshot of this visit, McBride's accepted *The Rivet in Grandfather's Neck* for publication in the autumn of that year, and *The Certain Hour* and *From the Hidden Way* for publication in 1916: but McBride's also, quite whole-heartedly, declined to sponsor any printing of *In the Flesh*.

This comedy was then put by, for some months, to make way for the publishing and the prompt failure of *The Rivet in Grandfather's Neck*. But in 1916 my typescript set forth once more a-travelling; and I find the itinerary to be succinct:

"Rejected by John Lane Company, in January 1916; by E. P. Dutton and Company, in March 1916; by Houghton Mifflin Company, in April 1916; by Charles Scribner's Sons, in June 1916;"

The record finishes just thus, with a semicolon, which one now finds rather pathetically defiant, through its implication that this is by no means to be the end. Nevertheless, I seem thereafter, for almost an entire year, to have squandered no more currency in express charges upon this unsalable typescript. . . . The particularly disheartening part, you see, was that even at McBride's, through whose unique optimism others of my books had met at last with editorial though not with financial favor, even there the opinion appeared unanimous with the opinions of all other publishing firms, that this special book was wholly null and virtueless.

WHAT happened next, I simply cannot say. I do not recall whether McBride's asked for another sight of this book or whether I again submitted it without waiting for any such invitation. Nor do I know for what reason the editorial staff of McBride's then altered their opinion as to *The Cream of the Jest*—as the story was now called,—beyond the fact that this changing can hardly have been caused by the firm's having published meanwhile three books by me, of which each had forthwith and utterly failed to "sell." But I do know that McBride's, in April 1917, accepted *The Cream of the Jest*, precisely two years after they had rejected it; and I find also that the John Lane Company brought out this book in England in 1923, some seven and a half years after the John Lane Company had rejected it. . . . The ways of all publishers, however, I discovered some while ago to be incalculable: and I do not think that any deduction can ever be drawn, through the channels of mere rationality, from any of their actions. It is perhaps the one trait which they share congenially with their authors.

The book was published, then, under its final title, *The Cream of the Jest*, in September 1917, and as a marketable product fell flat.

YET its publication had results. H. L. Mencken, that unusual and indeed unique youngster who, as you

may recall, had praised *The Cords of Vanity* some
eight or more years earlier, now came forth, in the
Smart Set, with a pleasingly polite article in which
The Cream of the Jest was appraised in combination
with a novel, quaintly entitled *The Three Black
Pennys*, lately published by a young Pennsylvanian.
This beginning novelist not long afterward came to
Dumbarton as a direct result of Mencken's article, so
that I first met Joseph Hergesheimer, just as I a bit
later met Mencken also, through virtue of having
published *The Cream of the Jest*.

Then also an even younger Burton Rascoe, who,
as yet in his early twenties, had but recently been
made literary editor of the Chicago *Tribune*, chanced
to be pleased by *The Cream of the Jest*; and he
forthwith decided that it was a book which should
not die unnoticed, at least not in Chicago. What I
take to have been the most remarkable, as it was
certainly the most rambunctious, of all campaigns in
the history of polite letters then opened, upon 29
December 1917, with the appearance, in the Chicago
Tribune, of an article by Burton Rascoe headed
"Here's a Chance to Own Another First Edition."
Thereafter, very much as the hapless Romans were
formerly assured by the elder Cato, in his every
public address upon whatsoever nominal theme, that
Carthage must be destroyed, so now, upon every
Saturday morning, all literate Chicago was assured
by Burton Rascoe that Cabell must be read.

The assertion did not pass unchallenged. Ben Hecht and Rupert Hughes, who ranked as well-thought-of writers in those times, were moved to comment upon my various books with fervor, and with all the good taste which either of these then prominent littérateurs possessed, in one or another of the Chicago papers. Through the pages of the *Herald-Examiner*, Vincent Starrett joined in, to commend *The Cream of the Jest*: B. L. T.'s Line-o'-Type column took up the matter of my literary demerits, in another section of the *Tribune* than was Rascoe's literary province, and in a rather more ribald vein: whereas Keith Preston and Richard Atwater waxed equally frank and derogatory in the Chicago *News*. And then,—as when upon some field of glory, the cold draft laws having fetched face to face the intrepid patriots of two nations, there the loud machine-gun answers to the ruthless speaking of its fellows ruthlessly,—so now did they who shared in this debate begin replying the one to another.

It all became quite learned, too, at the price of some lessening in coherence and in any exact meaning. Perhaps no one could ever have told you what all the printed rioting, and the tumultuary paragraphs, and the ungentle name-calling, were precisely about. I doubt if anybody much cared. But I know that Molière, and Menander, and Novalis, and Agathon, and Shakespeare, and Praxiteles, and Robert

W. Chambers, were all dragged somehow into the affair during the following months of insane dispute; and to each of these notabilities was accorded almost as much prominence in the various critical dicta as was being granted to me, now that Chicago had taken up polite letters in a really serious way. For some six months did the literati of Chicago thus debate whether I was an unjustly neglected author or a posturing imbecile. I became locally famous. Indeed I daresay a full hundred persons then living in Chicago must have known, vaguely, that somebody of my approximate name existed, and had published a book called something or other.

But the rest of America, so far as my publishers or I could perceive, remained deplorably oblivious of both facts: *The Cream of the Jest* appeared upon the "Marked Down" counters in all book stores: and yet two more years were to pass by before a book by me was to become a more or less salable commodity, in precisely that manner which in *The Cream of the Jest* I forecast and described with painstaking exactitude.

MEANWHILE I had heard again from that stripling Sinclair Lewis who had been the first of this book's so many rejectors. The intervening three years had so debased his literary standards that he now quite approved of *The Cream of the Jest*; thus we met before long, over the unfinished typescript of *Main Street*; and we got on together excellently. I found that, for my part, it was not possible to help liking and admiring this Sinclair Lewis, even after the droll and deferential boy whom I first knew had turned out to be a world-famous genius, owing deference to nobody and specializing in drolleries of a nature so caustic as to make his first letter to me of large monetary value.

So is it that, whenever I recall how through *The Cream of the Jest* I first met Lewis, and Hergesheimer, and Mencken, and Rascoe, and Guy Holt, I can see that in the end this book became, in some sense, the most potent of all my books in its influence upon my career as a writer. This book did not get for me any general recognition. It got for me, instead, something in every way more valuable. For it was *The Cream of the Jest* which first made for me, in the seventeenth year of my writing, a few warm friends who but a little later were to fight in my behalf very nobly, and with wholly heroic tenacity. . . . That, though, is not my present theme. I have not any need here to rehearse those now ancient battlings over *Jurgen*, which indeed had not anything in particular to do with *The Cream of the Jest*, and were not joined until 1920: but I have a strong need, and a never-dying urge, to record here, and to record upon every available occasion, my gratitude to all these and to yet other preservatory champions.

If few writers have met with more smug, more prurient, or more disingenuous opponents than chance has allotted me, no writer whatever, I think, has found more faithful allies. I now and then think also that, but for these allies, an almost-all-important personage would perhaps not ever have honored me with attention. I mean, of course, that "general reader" who in *The Cream of the Jest* becomes aware, on a sudden, of the existence of Felix Kennaston in just the same fashion in which "the author of *Jurgen*" was "discovered." I mean that but for that brave handful of persons who fought in *Jurgen's* behalf, the "general reader" would have heard no more about a quietly suppressed *Jurgen* than the "general reader" had ever heard, during the hope-deferring, failure-filled years before 1920, about my earlier books. And I deduce that, inasmuch as it was *The Cream of the Jest* which got for me so many of these friends and valiant benefactors, I may very well be but somewhat less grateful (upon equally un-literary grounds) to *The Cream of the Jest* than to them.

Straws and Prayer-Books

O F THIS *Straws and Prayer-Books* I have said in another place that it tells why the Biography of the Life of Manuel was written. That summary still seems valid and sufficient. None the less does it a bit awkwardly imply that any further commentary must appear superfluous, inasmuch as this comment cannot but take the form of explaining an explanation. I leave the point to precisians.

Meanwhile I remark that of all my publishings this volume may be declared to have enjoyed the least eventful history. The primordial notions for it came to its eventual writer very early in 1922, during the composition of A Note on Alcoves and of that Note's immediate postscript, The Appeal to Posterity,— which last-named paper in its final form is rechristened Flaws in the Spur. But not until November 1923 was actually begun the mental assembling of the materials for *Straws and Prayer-Books*, or, to be more exact, for "the Epilogue to the Biography," as in my thinking this yet untitled volume was cloudily indicated.

At this time, I started on the real composition of my Epilogue by outlining Romantics About Them and The Author of The Eagle's Shadow,—and also, when at this season I nominally reviewed the book *Fantastica* for the first issue of the *American Mercury*, by devoting the most of this review to observations upon certain myths which I intended to discuss later in my partially planned Epilogue, and to which I was to return yet again in *Something About Eve*. At this season, too, was discarded perforce my first notion of permitting John Charteris to deliver the Epilogue, as in *Beyond Life* he had spoken the Prologue, to the Biography of the Life of Manuel.

For it was soon apparent that I needed for "the Epilogue to the Biography" a new pattern, and a prose form which would be more catholic and more various than I, or in so far as I knew, anyone else had yet attempted. The form needed seemed a judicious compromise amidst *The Anatomy of Melancholy*, the Great Testament of Villon, the *Intentions* of Oscar Wilde, and the fairy tales of Hans Christian Andersen, with an infusion of George Moore's romanticizing egotism. It was not easy to construct any such form.

So for some six weeks' time did I mull over my outline, an outline which would symmetrically include in one all-embracing exposition (which I intended to intersperse refreshingly with dialogue) all the discursions and the several parables and the large paren-

theses such as seemed needful to explain my particular idea of "diversion,"—and which would also at
any moment permit an easy varying from one manner of writing to such another manner of writing as
more aptly fitted that subdivision of my many-faceted
theme then actually in hand. At the end of six weeks
this framework and this pattern were, in my mind,
complete. All, after that, became simple enough
going, now that the name of this volume also had
occurred to its author. So happily did affairs progress, indeed, that the physical putting together of
this book was begun during the last week of February 1924, and the completed typescript was delivered to its publishers during the following June.

FROM these publishers philanthropy had compelled
the discreet hiding of all knowledge as to "the new
book" save only its title. Publishers are, in their way,
long-suffering. They will now and then condone a collection of short stories or of essays, or even what
I have seen described as "a slender volume of verse,"
in their patient and heroic efforts to stay upon
friendly terms with the inconsiderate author who
invites them, through any of these dire agencies, to
court disaster. Yet I know not of that publisher who
could face with apparent equanimity the tidings that
one of his pampered writers was wasting typewriter

ribbons upon a volume in which the maniac planned to include book reviews.

It seems not possible anywhere to find readers for a volume of collected book reviews, if only because of that tone of unhuman certainty, and indeed of omniscience, which every reviewer of books is prompted to assume by all his better-thought-of models. While imposing enough in a brief dosage, this magisterial tone takes on an odd flavor of chuckle-headed and most drearily pompous asininity when it is maintained through an entire volume. Such at least is my theory as to the known fact that even the most widely revered of our literary critics are unable to vend their invaluable dicta in bulk.

I here was willing to be judged by the result, because it appeared to me that I had hit upon a rather novel prose form and a valid scheme,—a scheme whereunder Anatole France and Joseph Hergesheimer and George Moore marched equably with Tyl Ulenspiegel and John Charteris and Pan and the Queen of Elfhame. Yet I well knew that any outline of this scheme which mentioned the abhorred term "book reviews" could not but spread depression through the offices of Robert M. McBride & Company. So I hid away my secret half guiltily until *Straws and Prayer-Books* had been quite finished, to its last contrapuntal passage, and had then been polished off a bit, and after that had been behung

here and there with a half-dozen or so of yet other
verbal garlands.

THE book was published in November 1924. Although their inescapable task must have seemed not
wholly easy—to show that this *Straws and Prayer-
Books* also was but *Jurgen* all over again in a debased
form—yet many were the heroic souls among my
reviewers who flocked boldly to the attempt. I very
soon discovered, too, that I had, as people figura-
tively put it, my hands full, in the way of correspondents who had inferred that *Straws and Prayer-Books*
announced my intention to write no more books.
Some flatteringly protested against the assumed intention; others thought it a splendid if somewhat
belated bit of philanthropy. To all these correspondents I could but answer, as civilly as might be, that
Straws and Prayer-Books did not, to its author's
finding, announce any such present intention.

It has always been difficult for readers to comprehend that the various volumes of the Biography were
not being issued or written in their planned final
order, any more than had the chapters in any one of
these volumes (save only *The Eagle's Shadow*) been
composed in a sequence even remotely resembling
the order given them in the printed book. Every
writer must discover, through trial and error, that
method of composition which best suits, and which

most kindlily conceals from him, his deficiencies.
You may note that each writer does, by-and-by. For
my own part, I have always found it most convenient
to begin with what seemed to me the gist of the
writing I intended, working thence outwardly toward
the beginning and the end of its printed form. It thus
appears neatly symbolical that the earliest and the
lateliest written parts of each one of my books are
apt to occur somewhere toward the middle of the
volume, so that, even textually, I manage to end
about where I started.

THIS *Straws and Prayer-Books* strives to make clear
the causes which, to my opinion, underlie and prompt
the playing of every artist in letters. It, in any case,
tells you what prompted me to write the long Biography of the Life of Manuel. The thing was done
for, and in a special sense, my diversion.

That is the gist of all the pages in *Straws and
Prayer-Books*, that is the brief truism from which I
have worked outwardly. It may be that to admit this
truism is to plead guilty of the now unmodish misdemeanor of "art for art's sake." I do not know,
because, I confess, I have not ever been able to find
out what was meant by "art for art's sake"—although I have noticed, it is true, that this phrase is
never employed reprehendingly by anyone whom it

is possible for a merely human imagination to con-
nect with art.

Moreover, this volume serves as the Epilogue to,
and it thus actually completes, the Biography of the
Life of Manuel, upon the writing of which I began
in 1901, and the writing of which ended in 1929.
What follows is that when I look upon the finished
Biography, to-day, I cannot but wonder at the per-
tinacity with which this shelf-long romance has run
counter to every "literary trend" of the twenty-eight
years during which the Biography came to completion. It is a fact which, at all events as it touches the
case of one author, confirms me in my opinion about
the power and the interest of "literary trends,"—as
that opinion is stated in *Straws and Prayer-Books*, in
the remarks touching A Theme with Variations.

I continue to look back. . . . In that far-off 1901,
of course, all kinds of romanticism, when suitably
sterilized and sweetened, were well enough. Discreetly pastel-shaded Grünewalds and Ruritanias
ranked then as widely popular resorts: the historical
romance was everywhere a model of bad writing and
correct behavior, and a love-match was still, in every
book store, a panacea against all future ills. This
ended with surprising quickness. Overnight, as it
were, American novelists had turned *en masse* to
one or another aspect of what over-earnest young
persons still delight to call "the American scene";
and all better-thought-of writers who were heading

for oblivion by way of the American National Institute of Arts and Letters began everywhere to depict the immediate surroundings of their mental nonage, at first in the manner of an all-flatteringly retouched photograph, and, later, in the manner of a diatribe. One may find the earlier method still preserved by Mr. Booth Tarkington, quite innocuously, in a great many books of which I confess my enjoyment; whereas the practitioners of the second method appear too numerous, and upon the whole too unimportant, to be listed here or anywhere else with any least profit.

Meanwhile the Biography went on with the old paraphernalia of lovely words and of bright costumings and of long-obsolete quaint customs, and with the old poetic and chivalrous and gallant themes, and in particular with the old device of picaresque adventuring in unreal places. Fairhaven, for example, was invented as far back as 1902, although not much direct use was ever made of Fairhaven. Then Poictesme was discovered, in 1905; and steadily this Poictesme grew, as is elsewhere recorded. Lichfield also was established in 1906, for —as *The Cream of the Jest* has shown you, I hope —this Lichfield ranks in reality but as a suburb of Poictesme.

By-and-by Antan arose upon the horizon, inaccessibly: but Lytreia, and Puysange, and Lacre Kai, and Ecben, and Caer Omn, and Marna, and Rorn,

and Inis Dahut, and Sargyll, and Turoine, and Matocton, and Mispec Moor, and I know not how many
other places not as yet enregistered upon our stodgily
backward school maps, were visited one by one. And
the progeny of Manuel the Redeemer increased, too,
so that the perpetuated life of Dom Manuel now
blunderingly postured in all these thitherto unheard-of realms and cities, as my protagonist journeyed always—in the approved romantic manner
—about the improbable highways of bright lands
which were in nothing familiar; and the Biography
of the Life of Manuel was thus aggravated, page by
page, with additional chapters and with new volumes.

TO-DAY finds all this ended. The Biography has now
become, I believe, a completed and individual book.
In its architecture—as you may observe the aspiring
builder's plan to be more or less explicitly set forth
in my commentary on *The Line of Love*, because it
was from this volume that all the other volumes
grew—this longish book appears, to me, symmetrical. I, who am not unbiassed, think that in the Biography I have recorded how the life of Manuel has
journeyed upon what seemed to be the very woefully
long way between Storisende and Lichfield, only to
find out that, after all, the two places were as truly
sister cities as are St. Paul and Minneapolis; and
were severed, just as this last-named pair are severed,

but by a river. It is true that the dark and languid river which as yet divides Lichfield from Storisende is called Lethe.

I think that I have recorded, too, how, as the world grew more old and less forthright, my protagonist has changed, from within, unceasingly if subtly. The types, the three main types, in their essentials remain: but time has altered each one of them—unceasingly and subtly—as time alters all that which lives. Madoc, that undauntable poet who fetched his bride from behind the moon, and who got, if but for a scant while, the better of the Gray Three, has dwindled, by way of Villon and Wycherley and Gerald Musgrave, into a plump-bellied Felix Bulmer Kennaston, whose most prodigious exploits were the writing of a book or two. For that chivalrous-seeming Dom Manuel who once swaggered about the world of men, and who figured afterward, so they say, no less handsomely in that world which waits beyond every death-bed, could be found in our quiet Lichfield no analogue more exact than a Rudolph Musgrave who postured only in after-dinner speaking. And from the gallant copious sweep of Jurgen's adventuring my chronicle has perforce descended, through the long annals of Puysange, to the fidgeting and unsatisfying amours of Robert Etheridge Townsend. Like most other very old families, the Manuelites have learned to be urbane, and perhaps a bit more complex mentally, at the cost of diminishing both in the scope and the vigor of their doings.

MEANWHILE the Biography has become a completed and individual book,—a not meagrely planned book, in twenty parts, the biography of no one man, but a book which deals with the life of Manuel as that life has been perpetuated through some twenty-three generations. In every volume of the Biography that world-wandering life has been my protagonist. Time has altered my protagonist unceasingly and subtly; but only as time alters any other life. Fundamentally my protagonist does not change, in any one of my books; but remains, instead, under all temporal garbs and all surface stainings, very much the same blundering male ape, reft of his tale and grown rusty at climbing, forever aspiring but forever cautious, forever hungering for companionship and for comprehension and for sympathy, and yet, none the less, retaining forever inviolate that frigid and pale and hard, small core of selfishness which, as you may recall, Queen Freydis very long ago discovered—at the cost of heart-break—to be the heart of Manuel. . . . Yes: I am afraid that, at bottom, under every permissible human grace and large human gesture, and under each of my three human attitudes, that obscure slight heart-trouble has been perpetuated in

every one of the descendants of Manuel as ineradi-
cably as it yet endures in all the descendants of Adam.

Meanwhile the Biography has become a completed
and individual book. Its major theme I take to be the
democratic doctrine of our own world's Author, that
the average of one human life should not, or in
practice at least does not, differ appreciably from the
average of any other human life. . . . Since upon
this point I do not wish to appear dogmatic, I must
here refer you to the conclusions of Albert Aluys,
that extremely intelligent sorcerer whom Florian de
Puysange employed, in the nineteenth chapter of
The High Place, to evoke the more mighty and the
more lovely dead. . . . It follows that in every
incarnation the living of Manuel can but work out,
through not dissimilar situations and through very
much the same emotions, to very much the same
comedic ending upon, at happiest, a resignatory question mark. My protagonist sides, in brief, with
Rabelais and with Montaigne and with Socrates:
and at last can but echo, more or less variously, the
"Peut-être" and the *"Que sais-je?"* and the more
frank "I do not know" of these convinced and contented sceptics. . . . So is this eternal repetition
the strong connecting thread of the Biography, just
as this same eternal repetition has given solidarity
to all human living ever since men first discovered
those three great commonplaces which are called
love and marriage and death.

Meanwhile the Biography has become a completed
and individual book. And as such it must be judged,
whensoever it is judged. . . . You may not wisely
say, for example, that the Biography stresses over-
heavily its now obsolescent ideals and virtues. It is
true enough, of course, that *Domnei* exalts womanhood beyond our present-day, more prosaic beliefs,
and that *Jurgen* upholds the austere and strait-laced
and temporarily unpopular doctrine that a married
man had best remain faithful to his wife, just as it
is likewise true that *Something About Eve* depicts a
later Galahad who sets an example in the way of
male chastity such as not many of our younger gentry
as yet under seventy-five are inclined to follow of
their own will; and true also that *The Silver Stallion*
pleads frankly, with something it may be of the re-
vivalist's blunt stridor, for the sustaining faith of
old-fashioned religion. Yet these volumes touch upon
many other matters; the spiritual message of these
volumes is not wholly priggish: and, above all, the
contents of any one volume may now fairly claim
their right to be weighed in their just proportion to
the entire Biography.

Equally you must not declare that the Biography
depends upon sexual antics, quite as utterly as mere
human life depends upon these quaint exercises, to
secure its continuance; or, at any rate, you should
not say this until after any such parts of the Biography as may seem to you to hunt the beast with two

backs have been fairly weighed in their proportion
to the entire Biography. You will then find, I think,
that the proportion is about the same discreetly edited
ratio which is displayed, one regrets to note, not in
human action but through the more timid medium of
this morning's newspaper.

WHAT it all comes to is, that I believe one would
wiseliest advance no more sweeping or more general
statements as to the Biography than the judicious will
advance concerning human life. For I believe that—
here, too—"realism" has conquered, in so far that,
in a sort of allegoric shorthand, I have written a very
long book which is "true to life." I believe that the
Biography, when judged as a whole, does summarize,
in tolerably correct proportion, the main elements
of our average human living: and I believe also that
the Biography has now earned its right to be judged
not piecemeal but as a whole.

I believe, in fine, that the Biography is a completed and individual book which depicts, in depicting the Life of Manuel, the Life of Man. It is in
this faith—which is, no doubt, as erroneous as all
other human faiths—that I elect to take leave of the
Biography, and of my twenty-eight years' playing
with it.

The NOTES

"*The honorablest part of talk is to vary speech of the present occasion with arguments, tales with reasons, asking of questions with telling of opinions, and jest with earnest: for it is a dullard's work to jade anything too far.*"

A Note Upon Poictesme

WHEN I came to preface the illustrated edition of *The Silver Stallion*, I found myself in the position, not altogether unexampled to human experience, of noting that affairs in this inexplicable world of ours sometimes fall out a bit quaintly . . . For I regarded those soul-contenting pictures which Mr. Papé had just completed, at his home in Tunbridge Wells, to adorn the pages of this the lateliest written, and the last, of all the stories of Poictesme. I thought about the yet other illustrations—in *Jurgen*, and in *Figures of Earth*, and in *Domnei*, and in *The High Place*, and in *The Cream of the Jest*,—which had been coming, year after year, from Mr. Papé's studio, on St. John's Road in Tunbridge Wells, to represent Poictesme as a land of such never-failing loveliness and drollery as I have found but too often to be humiliatingly absent from the accompanying text. And I recalled how my own less scintillant province, the Poictesme of the text, came out of this same Tunbridge Wells as long ago as 1905,— "*bonæ sub regno Cynaræ,*" Theodore being Consul.

243

NOBODY need believe in the coincidence. I do not
quite believe in it myself. None the less, I can well
remember how when I was writing *Gallantry* the
characters perforce all went to Tunbridge Wells and
spent the earlier half of my book there, and thus
landed me—who then had not ever visited this water-
ing place—in endless difficulties. Map and histories
are all very well: but they do not comfortably suffice
in dealing with a town which you have never seen,
and which still endures to confute you . . . Meanwhile, to every side, problems arose. Upon which
of the hills would Lady Allonby have lodged in 1750?
just where would Captain Audaine have fought his
duels? what was, in 1750, the dubious quarter of the
town to which a profligate nobleman would abduct
an heiress? into what suburbs would Vanringham
most naturally have eloped with his Marchioness?
and at what inn would the great Duke of Ormskirk
have sought accommodation when he came down
from London to dispose of the Jacobite conspiracy?
Such were but five of the hundred or so niggling problems which fretted my imaginary stay in Tunbridge
Wells; which made mere maps and histories inadequate; and which caused me to resolve for the remainder of the book, and indeed for the remainder
of my auctorial career, to deal with a geography less
prodigally adorned with doubts and pitfalls.

Never again, when any possible option is at hand,
I said, will I lay the scene of any story in a real place.

And I have held faithfully to that saying. Of the books written since 1905, none has paid the least tribute, in point of fact, to the fixed laws or to the shapings of a world contrived by any other demiurge than myself.

SO WHEN Ormskirk had disposed of his English imbroglios, and when he quitted the Wells, to our shared relief, and when he went into France to visit incognito his betrothed wife, then Mr. Bulmer's first meeting with Mademoiselle de Puysange occurred in a byway of Louis Quinze's kingdom thitherto unknown to cartographers. It was at this time, in the final months of 1905, that Poictesme was born—of an illicit union between Poictiers and Angoulême,— and that a rejuvenescent John Bulmer discovered this province. It was then that the château of Bellegarde was erected, and the forest of Acaire was planted, to suit the needs of John Bulmer's story. Upon the horizon the Taunenfels arose, to afford Achille Cazaio an appropriate residence; the Duardenez river flowed coyly just into sight; and somewhere in the background, I gathered from the conversation of them whom John Bulmer met in Poictesme, were Manneville and Des Roches and Beauséant.

This much alone of Poictesme then came into being, this tiniest snippet of the land then sprouted, as it were, out of my trouble with Tunbridge Wells;

and this much of the province served me at this period, quite adequately, through the episode called In the Second April.

Poictesme availed me yet again as I went on with *Gallantry*, and wrote, in 1906, the episode called The Scapegoats, which (in addition to exploiting the kindred realm of Noumaria) established a bit more definitely the existence of the town of Manneville . . . But by this time I was fairly caught. No author lately escaped from all that trouble in Tunbridge Wells could resist the attractions of a land so cour-teous in providing out of hand for its historian's least need in the way of inns and cities and forests, and not even boggling over the instant erection of a mountain range wherever it would come in most serviceably. So the town in which Nelchen Thorn had just been murdered by Monsieur de Gâtinais was immediately visited by Prince Edward Longshanks and Ellinor of Castile,—which couple, in travelling from Northern France into Spain, conducted a tenson in this same Manneville, as is duly recorded in *Chivalry*. Thus casually was the province of Poic-tesme fixed in the southern section of France, on the road to Castile; and thus casually came two of my books to deal, more or less, with Poictesme.

THERE Poictesme rested until 1910, when *Domnei* was started. And then, with this obliging province

standing ready, with this whole realm at hand
wherein no blunders in any point of fact or in any
geographical detail were humanly possible, then quite
inevitably the story of *Domnei* began in Poictesme;
and yet further civic additions were made, in Montors and Fomor. A little later Felix Kennaston ex-
plored this so convenient nook of old-world France,
during the composition of *The Cream of the Jest* in
1914; and it was he who first heard of Naimes and
Bovion and Perdigon and Lisuarte, and who came
as a pioneer to the castle of Storisende. It was he
also who during 1914 found embodied in Horvendile
a most useful notion which the author of *Gallantry*,
in dealing with Francis Vanringham, had weighed
and found unembodiable in 1905.

But far more important, to me at least, was this
Felix Kennaston's discovery that Poictesme was "a
land wherein human nature kept its first dignity and
strength, and wherein human passions were never in
a poor way to find expression with adequate speech
and action." That discovery—again, to me at least—
touched upon what I have since found to be the special feature of this province. Poictesme is a land
wherein almost anything is rather more than likely
to happen save one thing only: it is not permissible
in Poictesme for anybody to cease, for one moment,
from remaining a human being or ever to deviate
from human sanity . . . From human speech, yes:
for in Poictesme, I grant you, one does avoid the

poor flat colloquialisms with which men and women as yet parody their thoughts and emotions; in Poictesme one expresses these thoughts and emotions as handsomely and as accurately as may be. That this is not "true to life" I have heard; yet I do not think that any man becomes appreciably less vital when he stops stuttering . . . Now in thus adhering to human sanity Poictesme of course follows the old laws of faëry rather than the best rules of modern literature; for as Mr. Gilbert Chesterton has observed:

"The problem of fairy tales is—what will a healthy man do with a fantastic world? The problem of the modern novel is—what will a madman do with a dull world? In the fairy tales the cosmos goes mad; but the hero does not go mad. In the modern novel the hero is mad before the book begins, and suffers from the harsh steadiness and cruel sanity of the cosmos."

Well, and so is it in the fairy-haunted world of Poictesme; its people remain healthy and rational among circumstances howsoever surprising. I mean in other words very much what Mr. H. L. Mencken has declared concerning the various legends of Poictesme:

"What gives them, as documents, their peculiar tartness is the fidelity of their realism. Their gaudy heroes, in the last analysis, chase dragons precisely as stockbrokers play golf. Is Jurgen, even when be-

fore the great God Pan, superbly real? Then it is
because he remains a Rotarian in the depths of that
terrible grove. Is Manuel? Then it is because what
he hopes and suffers and achieves in Poictesme is
substantially identical with what Felix Kennaston
hopes and suffers and achieves in Lichfield."

SO, THEN, did Poictesme continue to sprout out of
the trouble which Tunbridge Wells had caused me:
and *The Cream of the Jest* thus added its large quota
to the laws and to the geography, and to the past,
of this province.

Thereafter I followed Jurgen's adventuring,
throughout the greater part of 1918: and the lay of
Poictesme was now sufficiently known for a map to
be made of it. Yet *Figures of Earth* and *The High
Place* and *Straws and Prayer-Books* and *The Silver
Stallion* were each later to add here and there to the
land's physical features, until finally, in 1925, in the
pages of *The Silver Stallion*, the very last settlements
were effected, at St. Tara and St. Didol. My final
visit to Poictesme during 1928, in *The White Robe*,
established no more towns, nor any new discovery
except the worth-noting fact that Poictesme was so
far in advance of all other French provinces that its
judges wore wigs during the first years of the seventeenth century. Meanwhile the history of Poictesme,
between the years 1234 and 1750, had been revealed

to me: and the land, so far as I myself may presume
to act as a judge, had become real.

Never again, I had said, will I lay the scene of any
story in a real place. So I invented Poictesme: and
thereupon—for such, again, was the quaint fashion
in which affairs fell out—Poictesme rebelliously became a real place.

At least it seems to me a real place, nowadays, by
every known rule of logic. I find Poictesme is duly
listed in modern dictionaries and similar books of
reference. The maps attributed to Koch and Bülg
and Borsdale present the province in three different
stages of civilization. Its longitude is now definitely
known to have been just four degrees east, although
its latitude, to be sure, has been disputed, as too
largely moral. Each one of its leading personages
has been commemorated in a biography; the land's
history is upon public record; its laws and legends
have been summarized; the development of its religion is known; a considerable section of its literature has been preserved; in at least one symphony
and in a fair number of songs its music endures; and
its relics in the way of drawings and paintings and
mural decorations and sculpture are still tolerably
numerous.

As for the bibliography of Poictesme, it now rivals
in bulk that of any other French province. You have
but to compare Poictesme with Chalosse, for example, or with Amont, or with Grasivaudan, or with

Quercy, or with Velay, to see how little has been
written about any one of these provinces in comparison with what has been written about Poictesme.
These other provinces have found but partial and
infrequent historians, in publications not ever very
widely known: whereas a host of notable and diverse
savants—such as Gottfried Johannes Bülg, and Carl
Van Doren, and John Frederick Lewistam, and H. L.
Mencken, and Paul Verville, and John S. Sumner,
and La Vrillière, and Hugh Walpole, and John
Macy, and the Rev. Fathers of the College of St.
Hoprig, and I know not how many other erudite persons, have increased the bibliography of Poictesme,
year after year, from every conceivable point of
view.

So is it that, when once you have ventured into
logic, the evidence for the reality of such famous
realms as Sumeria and Troy and Carthage, and of
Philistia itself, appears less multifariously established than is the reality of Poictesme. So is it that
when, in Pliny, let us say, I read of such once notable
places as Tacompsos (by some called Thaticê), and
of Gloploa, and of Rhodata, where a golden cat was
worshipped as a god, and of the pleasant island kingdom of Hora, and of Orambis (so curiously situated
upon a stream of bitumen), and of Molum, which
the Greeks, as you will remember, called Hypaton,
—that I then, of course, believe in the reality of
every one of these places as vouched for by Roman

science, but that, even so, upon the whole, I think
the proofs to be more numerous and more clear, to-
day, for the existence of Poictesme.

Piety prevents me from dwelling upon the claims
of this province to be believed in as an actual place,
as compared with the more shadowy claims of lands
for whose former existence we have, none the less,
the irrefutable warrant of Holy Writ. I say only
that to me this land of Poictesme appears as real
and as readily accessible a country as the land of
Temani, or as the land of Erez, or as the land of
Shinar,—wherein, as every Sunday-schoolboy knows,
the great Emperor Nimrod ruled over Accad and
Erech and Babel and yet other dependencies . . . In
fine, I have come to believe in the family-tree of the
Counts of Poictesme as completely as I do in that
of the Dukes of Edom. And that Bellegarde and
Montors and Storisende were once real cities in this
actual land standing midway between Montpellier
and Castries seems to me as thoroughly demonstrated
as that Reheboth and Nineveh and Resen once stood
midway between Calneh and Calah.

And I find it droll enough to reflect that all these
things were created, not wholly and on a sudden, as
in *The Silver Stallion* the young Ænseis create their
own worlds to play with, but, rather, as though all
these things had sprouted, a little by a little, out of
the trouble which Tunbridge Wells once caused me.
I gratefully recognize that for some twenty-five years

Poictesme was to me a never-failing source of diversion and, at times, of active delight. Without any
such sure elation do I recognize also that for some
twenty-five years I lived in Poictesme, as went all
practical and serious intents, with occasional, brief,
rather hurried trips abroad to visit my family and
a few merely physical intimates.

IN ANY case, there will be no more stories about
Poictesme. And, as I said at outset, it seems queer,
whensoever I appraise the large host of Mr. Papé's
pictures which have come out of Tunbridge Wells to
establish yet more clearly the existence of Poictesme
—yes, it seems very queer, to reflect how prodigally
has Tunbridge Wells atoned to me for the troubles
which Tunbridge Wells once created.

Addenda as to Jurgen

LESS is the trouble that through any change of mind I wish now to write a definite commentary as to *Jurgen* than is the shock attendant upon the discovery that I have already done so. In my hands lies a copy of Burton Rascoe's *Prometheans*; and by an odd coincidence, such as few authors will find to be unexampled, I had turned first to an article which seemed to be about me.

So, on a sudden, do I find the learned author of *Prometheans* quoting in full a letter which I wrote him during the summer of 1919 in reply to his questions about how I came to work out the ideas and the construction of *Jurgen*? and what in brief had been in my mind the book's genesis?

Now at this time, as I must ask you to remember, *Jurgen* had not been published. Burton and I, having read it only in typescript, did not know that in print *Jurgen* could be regarded as a lewd story. Only in regard to the book's origins had been the questions that I had answered in this letter, the writing of which—upon the front porch of our cottage at the

Rockbridge Alum Springs, on a pearl gray morning
—I did now remember clearly enough, without being
able in the least to recollect what this letter contained.
The author of *Prometheans* had not asked my con-
sent to include in his book this letter which, if I had
ever thought about it at all, I would have believed
to have perished long since. He had thus laid himself open, I am told, to several thousands of dollars
—or perhaps it was hundreds of thousands of dollars
—in the way of damages, from which I may or may
not absolve him eventually. My point here is but that
to discover, without any least warning, in a printed
book you have honorably bought and paid for, a
rather long letter which you wrote some fifteen years
earlier—without any least thought of its publication
—is sufficiently startling.

So I read with a lively interest this letter, which
on 10 August 1919 began abruptly enough:

"It was a year ago last March that I temporarily
put aside my *Something About Eve*, to write for
Mencken the short story he requested and seemed
to merit. I evolved then very much the same Some
Ladies and Jurgen in imagination as eventually appeared in the *Smart Set*: wherein the devil offers
Jurgen the three symbolic ladies, Guenevere and
Cleopatra and Helen, and the poet prefers, upon the
whole, his prosaic wife. But as I wrote it out, I
scented possibilities. How much more effective, for

instance, it would be if Jurgen had previously known
and loved and lost these women.

"Of course, that meant to me a dizain, with four
tales already suggested. It would be out of space
and time, of necessity, if Jurgen were to encounter
these three who lived centuries apart. So, with my
story still unwritten, I began to plan the dizain, of
ten short stories, to be disposed of severally for much
fine gold.

"Ah, but the Cleopatra episode! Here I foresee
myself heading straight for an imitation of *Aphrodite* and Louys' notion of life in Alexandria. Well,
then, let us substitute the goddess herself in place
of the Cleopatra who symbolizes her, and call the
goddess—no, not Aphrodite, because the Grecianisms
must be reserved for the Helen part. I consider her
other names, and am instantly captivated by the
umlaut in Anaïtis."

It is at this point that I groan aloud. Did I actually
write "umlaut" where any tolerably well educated
person would have written "diæresis"? No doubt I
did: but in that case Rascoe (confound him) ought
to have corrected the error before printing my letter.
I decide to consult with my lawyer about bringing
suit; and I continue my reading.

"So my second heroine becomes Anaïtis, a moon
goddess. But her lovers are solar legends . . . Why,
to be sure! For does not Guenevere typify the spring?
Anaïtis summer? and Helen, in her Leukê avatar,

the autumn? I perceive that Jurgen is a solar legend —and inevitably spends the winter underground. There is the Hell episode postulated, then.

"I make out my calendar, and find it 37 days short, since obviously the year must be rounded out. Where was Jurgen between 22 March and 30 April? The question answers itself; and I spy the chance to use that fine idea, which has been in my mind for fifteen years or more, as to how Heaven was created.

"I am getting on now, with my dizain lacking only three episodes—since the half-written magazine story has obviously split into an opening and an ending of a book. (That is, I, thus far, think it the ending.) And now I am wondering if there is not a chance at last for that other fine idea I could not ever find a place to work into—the going back to a definite moment in one's past."

I pause here, aghast. After all, I was supposed to be writing in English. By-and-by I guess the enigma to mean that I was wondering if there were not a chance to work into *Jurgen* the "fine idea" of going back to a definite moment in one's past and of thence beginning life all over again, an idea which (it seems) I had turned over in my mind before 1918, but had not thitherto found an opportunity to include in my writings. With that settled, and with a few more maledictions despatched Rascoe-ward, for not having permitted me to edit this letter before he published it, I continue to read about this idea **of** going back to a definite, a well remembered moment in one's past. I find my namesake, some fifteen years earlier, upon the front porch of a cottage at the now perished Rockbridge Alum Springs, to be asking, in regard to the purpose of this going back:

"For what?—obviously, for a woman, since Jurgen has by this time taken form as a person . . . What woman, though?—why, clearly, the woman who in his youth represented the never quite attainable Helen. And she was Count Emmerick's second sister, whose existence I had postulated in *The Jest* with the intention of using her in due time.

"I christen her Varvara, in general consonance with my Russian Koshchei—who, I am beginning to perceive, must be more than a mere devil if the book is to ascend . . . Yes, he must be the Demiurge, and God his creation . . . Then Koshchei must be rather stupid, and not be bothering himself about Jurgen at all. I need, therefore, another supernatural agent, some one more near to purely human affairs, to direct Jurgen's wanderings. My mind being already on Russian mythology, and the regaining of a lost day being involved, the Léshy, who according to Russian folklore control the days, present themselves; and I select Sereda for Jurgen to wheedle out of, of course, one of the Wednesdays when he was young. Another episode.

"But this Varvara—no, nobody will be certain as to the pronunciation of Varvara. Call her Dorothy."

It is here that once more I desist from reading.
This letter runs far too glibly. Though it does not say
outright, yet it none the less implies, that Varvara
was thus changed on a sudden into Dorothy la Désirée, while the book was being outlined; but in fact,
as I very well know, she remained Varvara until
the book was virtually finished. Yet this small point
is not of importance, I decide; and I continue
reading.

"This Dorothy, then, will disappoint him—a little,
anyhow—if he goes back to the actual girl. Really
to go back, he must return to the girl as she seemed
to him, and he must himself be young again. Yet the
point is already in my mind that, while Jurgen is to
keep the youth which would come back to him with
the replevined Wednesday, so far as his body goes,
still his mind is to remain middle-aged. I grope to
the ironic scheme of letting him win to his ideal girl
as he actually is—and so be to her, of course, un-
recognizable.

"Then he must somehow get rid of his false youth
before his interview with Koshchei in the cave."

This inference does not seem clear. Then I remember that an interview between a middle-aged
poet and a putative devil was the germ from which
everything began. I perceive what I was talking
about,—which is always a comfort. I meant that, in
order to preserve my starting point in composition,
it was necessary for Jurgen, in some manner or an-

other, to become middle-aged once more, before the
now almost completely planned book could reach the
actual starting point of its existence as a book, in
the "situation" from which I first began to work out
Jurgen.

I am mildly pleased. This seems to me a most excellent illustration of the "method"—of which I
spoke in my commentary upon *Straws and Prayer-
Books*—of commencing with the gist of a book and
of working thence to the beginning and the end of its
printed form. As in the forty chapters of *Figures of
Earth* thirty-four, so in the fifty chapters of *Jurgen*
forty-three, are but preliminary matter to the notion
with which I started the book and from which the
entire book developed. And here is the fifteen-year-
old proof of it.

With that settled, I continue to read what remains
of my letter.

"The getting rid of this false youth makes for me
the tenth episode . . . No; I still lack the machinery
for getting him to the Garden where he encounters
young Dorothy. A Centaur appears the handiest
method of combining transportation and conversation. I think inevitably of Nessus, then of his shirt.
Yes, something must be done with that shirt. And
that episode must come first, while Jurgen is still
middle-aged.

"Well, there you are. That is about how the outline of the book came to me : and at this stage I went

back to the *Smart Set* story and actually wrote it.
Thereafter I set about writing my ten episodes (and
found them resolutely determined not to be short
stories, on any terms); and rewrote them; and put
in, here and there, just anything which occurred to
me; and changed this, and altered that; and groped
to that loathsome last chapter, as the tale's inevitable
ending. And almost last of all, I pivoted the whole
thing upon the shadow and the shirt, which were
almost the last things of all I thought of. So, you
see, the book virtually wrote itself."

That is all there is of my letter—or in any event
that is all which Rascoe printed, and all with which
I am nowadays conversant.

I REGARD it wistfully. If only I had known that this
letter existed when in 1928 I wrote for the Storisende
edition the all-dodging commentary upon *Jurgen*
which is printed elsewhere, then I could have worked
over this rather horribly phrased and far too elliptic
letter into a most excellent commentary. For it is all
first-hand information; it recorded, virtually at the
moment of their happening, affairs which I have
now forgotten long ago,—recording them too without any tinge of special pleading, inasmuch as this
letter was written to a well-trusted friend with no
thought of its publication; and above all, it is untarnished with any notion that anybody could think

Jurgen to be "indecent." Since 1920 that notion has cast me, willy-nilly, in the rôle of attorney for the defence whensoever I had to refer to *Jurgen*; and I do not doubt my enforced position has colored my speaking.

But here you have my inedited commentary upon this book, just as I put down upon paper the mental genesis of *Jurgen* at a time when there was no question of defending this book against charges of any nature. I rejoice to have this commentary, as in some sort a yet further exoneration of my original intentions, to which I referred in prefacing the Storisende edition of *Jurgen*. But I do wish, from the grieved bottom of my heart: (*a*) that I could have seen this letter a bit sooner, before I wrote my more formal commentary; and (*b*) that before this letter was printed I had been permitted to touch up its phraseology.

A Little More About Eve

SOMETHING ABOUT EVE is a book which concerns itself (as indeed its title indicates) peculiarly with women, I reflected when I came to preface the illustrated edition of this romance; and it so raised what has become with me a delicate topic. A Southerner is very often and quite easily shocked, but especially in any matter which touches chivalry.

For this reason I am frequently upset to an unbelievable degree when people tell me, as they do over and over again, with rather maddening unanimity, that women have not been fairly dealt with in that collection of my books which make up the Biography of Dom Manuel's perpetuated life upon earth . . . Yet other persons, to be sure, profess that women are introduced into the Biography solely in order that men may deal fairly with them in Jurgen's personal application of this phrase. Either way, there seems a general feeling—particularly awkward for a Southern author to be encountering—that, throughout my books, this half of the world's population has been neglected if not actually slandered.

After due confession that this is quite possibly
true, I confess I do not think it is true. I must point
out that women, in common with all other non-human
creatures such as gods and fiends and ghosts, appear
in the Biography only as this one or the other of them
seems to this or that human, and therefore, of course,
to this or that very easily deceived, male person. I
must point out that the point of view of the Biography is always masculine. I must remind you, in
brief, that I have attempted no actual or complete
portrait of any woman anywhere; but only a depiction of some man's notions about one or another
woman.

To this rule there are but two exceptions, I believe,
throughout the entire Biography—in "Sweet Adelais" and in Porcelain Cups—wherein for technical
reasons all is necessarily seen through a young girl's
lustrous and youth-blinded eyes. Elsewhere I have
self-confessedly rendered some other man's notion
of some woman,—whether this other man's all-tinc-
turing nature were a medium so heavily or so slightly
encoloring whatever it transmits as I have variously
employed in Nicolas de Caen and in Richard Harrowby and in Gottfried Johannes Bülg and in Robert
Etheridge Townsend and in Captain Francis Audaine
and in the anonymous redactors of the legends of
Poictesme. All these speak "in character"; but all
remain male.

It follows that everywhere I have but recorded one

or another more or less individualized male's notion
about an especial woman, as a notion for the correctness of which I could assume no responsibility. And
I find it droll to note that, because of my super-
abundant cautiousness whensoever I came to deal
with women, in all the many thousands of pages
which I have written, just thrice—once in The Story
of the Choices, and once in *Domnei*, and once in *The
Rivet in Grandfather's Neck*—are two women ever
left alone together, and the mystery is briefly guessed
at, how they behave when no man is present? Well,
and even then it is not I, but Nicolas de Caen and
Richard Harrowby, who attend severally to this
guess-work.

I have preferred to err, where error appeared inevitable, upon the less ludicrous side. Reading any
printed narrative by a woman wherein the authoress
—for at this precise point all female writers become
mildly quaint "authoresses"—purports to render for
you the interior being of any male character, then
the male reader cannot but become puzzled and just
vaguely perturbed. The teddied creatures are clever.
They, whose empirical knowledge is complete, do
understand us—almost. But, after all, nothing in the
picture is really quite right. The most gifted of
women writers, in dealing with an ostensibly male
character from the inside, seems but to contrive one
of those "artistic" photographs in which not any special feature but merely everything is slightly out of

focus. I can recall not one instance in which since the world began to be pestered with authorship any woman writer has depicted a man even fairly credible, to her male readers, when once she had reversed the intentions of nature by trying to penetrate the man's exterior.

Well, and since they understand us far better than we do them, I can but deduce that when a male writer attempts to depict a woman from within, it is with an even more heavy emphasis that he then makes a fool of himself. I refrain from at least that single form of folly. I present, throughout the whole Biography, those women and gods and fiends and fabulous monsters which enter thereinto, only as they appear to some especial male, because that, after all, is the sole point of view from which I or any other man can ever regard any of these myth-enveloped beings.

—WHICH reminds me, through no instantly apparent connection, of my daily correspondence. There are, I now and then hopefully imagine, no more persons remaining anywhere in the United States of America sufficiently interested in the correct pronunciation of my surname to write and ask me about it: then the postman comes to confute optimism, and upon the following Saturday I must type off two or three more statements that "Cabell" rhymes with "rabble." But almost if not quite so often does the postman bring an inquiry as to what was the really fundamental explanation of one or another phenomenon witnessed by Manuel, or by Jurgen or Florian or Gerald, or by some other of my leading male Manuelites; and, in brief—through that sempiternal assumption that all art is a branch of pedagogy,—what parable, what allegoric teaching did I intend by the passage in question? What, here to employ the usual phrase, does this or that passage in the Biography of the Life of Manuel "mean"?

Then, on the following Saturday, I must type off a confession of more or less humiliating ignorance. I must explain that I have but recorded from the point of view of one or another special male that which he witnessed. I have told the reader, for example, what Manuel saw and heard, or I have set down all that Florian or Jurgen or Gerald ever knew about some particular matter: and concerning this same matter that is all which I myself can pretend to know. In short, I refer my correspondent to a book called *Special Delivery*, with a thrifty hint that he or she would do well to purchase a copy and thus find under the heading Mirror and Pigeons the whole point discussed at a length unpermissible in a letter. To these sentiments, in one or another wording, I then subscribe myself, upon Saturday after Saturday, Yours faithfully.

After that, I try to fold my note so as to fit it

neatly into the stamped and self-addressed envelope
which was thoughtfully enclosed by my correspondent, and I find that never by any chance is the
achievement possible. It appears that, through a truly
remarkable coincidence, the more inquisitive of
American novel readers, in common with most collectors of autographs, all deal with the same sta-
tioner, who purveys a very special sort of envelope
so abbreviated lengthwise as to accommodate not
any known size of writing paper.

But I divagate. My point is, that just so do women
rank in the Biography. I can but tell you all that my
protagonist, in each especial volume, ever knew about
them, and as a rule that was not much.

YET it may be that there is a second reason for this
gingerly handling of women, as concerns at least
their unphysical aspects. It may be that, even nowadays and despite the gray horrors of my embitter-
ment, I still remain too much the romantic ever to
regard women as human beings . . . For one has
the assurance of the very best-thought-of critics that
"the author of *Jurgen*"—whom I privately tend to
disesteem as a semi-fabulous creature—is "an embittered romantic." He began, it seems, by writing
the most philanthropic, if somewhat overblown and
cloying tales, in his far-away youth: but, with ad-
vancing age, he found the world not altogether that

which he had expected it to be, and so lost his temper,
and began to be dreadfully peevish about affairs in
general. He seems to have been completely upset by
the shock. Never, it appears, has "the author of
Jurgen" quite got over his soul-shattering discovery,
—with the result that, week after week, the returns
from the clipping bureau have brought me the most
authoritative information as to this embittered romantic existing in a never-lifting atmosphere of despair and frustration . . . And one resignedly accepts the label, because, after all, every writer of
some years' standing has to be classified, by those
who are both younger and more certain about everything than he can ever hope to become again.

The great trouble is that this labeling does a bit
complicate private life. Nobody, with any real comfort to himself, can go on being an embittered romantic twenty-four hours to the day when so many
pleasant things are continually happening. It would
call for more self-control than seems reasonable. Besides, if I dared to try out the rôle of an embittered
romantic in the home circle, and among those surroundings in which the major part of my life is
passed, everyone would be surprised and upset. In
fact, the family physician would be sent for. So upon
the very rare occasions that I provisionally attempt
to live up to the standards of the best-thought-of
critics, by acting as befits an embittered romantic,

then the thing has to be done when the presence of company has temporarily stilled the frankness of connubial comment.

Even so, when you first meet strangers, and particularly interviewers, the situation becomes faintly embarrassing. You feel the weight of fine social obligations; you feel that these aliens at least may expect you to behave as an embittered romantic, and that they may even have some assured information, denied to you, as to how an embittered romantic does behave; and in consequence you are confused about just what to say. You can but desperately attempt to hide behind a look of friendly yet cynical amusement; and to assume an air of thinking the most superior thoughts very well suited for publication in the *New Republic* or in any of the better-class college magazines. And you feel too that you are bungling the whole affair . . . No; it is not easy for an embittered romantic to maintain the appropriate atmosphere of despair and frustration in his private and social life, with any real comfort to himself.

—All which is a bit afield. I had meant only to say that a romantic, even when of the embittered variety, perhaps cannot ever, quite, regard women as human beings.

NOW, to do this is, of course, the signal attempt of the twentieth century,—to regard women as human

beings. I am not sure the experiment will succeed: but
the outcome, after all, I take to be no concern of mine,
whereas I am certain I have found it drolly interesting to observe the progress of Eve's daughters.

For a great while they were but conveniences,
equally for housework and copulation. Then, as the
more talented courtesans were evolved, women here
and there began to be ranked among the luxuries
and adornments of life, exactly as we of late have
seen yet other bed-chamber and kitchen furnishings,
under the name of Early Americana, turned into
prized ornaments of the drawing-room.

But the apex was reached in the mediæval notion
of domnei—perhaps the most aspiring, and very
certainly the most unpredictable, of all the many in-
ventions of romanticists—whereby women became
goddesses, in that they were reverenced as the most
pure and lovely symbols of Heaven to be found anywhere upon earth. Of this domnei I have written
sufficiently in another place. Yet I must here point
out that domnei was always a cult limited in its membership to the upper classes; and that every avowal
of its proud faith was limited, too, as if instinctively,
to the golden, pleasurably befogging, fine mists of
poetry. Side by side with domnei, as the main trend
of mediæval prose literature shows very plainly, per-
sisted always the monkish notion of woman as a snare
of the devil, and the bourgeois notion of woman as

a false and lustful animal. The romanticist, that is, tended, as he still tends, howsoever timidly, to be a gentleman. Domnei prevailed only among the gentry, among those who had the leisure, and the good taste, to play with what Gerald Musgrave calls "a rather beautiful idea."

Well, and now, as a part perhaps of the quite general discrediting of all gentle notions everywhere, as a bit overflavored with fudge, now this ends. To every side of us, the lady—a word which is so significant that to record the four letters of it here must permeate this whole page with old-fashionedness—the lady, I observe, is triumphantly climbing down to full equality with the butler and the truck driver. I daresay, inasmuch as I have Madame Melior de Puysange to back me, that the pedestal upon which domnei exalted every gentlewoman had its discomforts . . . The lady, in any event, grows nowadays as rare as the horse; these two, who were formerly the dearliest prized chattels of every well-bred male, now race neck and neck toward extinction: and the progress of all women's evolution into human beings appears quaint and edifying. Yet I watch it with auctorial disinterest, for with the decadence of gentlewomen the Biography of the Life of Manuel has no concern. The Biography treats of more backward days when this common-sense metamorphosis had hardly, if at all, begun.

I CONFESS, in brief, that the male inheritors of Manuel's life—from whose point of view I have written that Biography which makes me an embittered romantic every Thursday, when the envelope from the clipping bureau comes in,—that these Manuelites, throughout the Biography, have approached the daughters of Eve with an underlying feeling of unintimacy. And now occurs to me yet a third reason for this confessed fact.

I would suggest that the inheritors of Manuel's life were perhaps the victims of heredity. For it was Manuel himself, as you may remember, who remarked upon Upper Morven, at the height of his love-affair with Queen Freydis:

"What can I ever be to you except flesh and a voice? I know that my distrust of all living creatures —oh, even of you, dear Freydis, when I draw you closest—must always be as a wall between us, a low, lasting, firm-set wall which we can never pull down. There is no way in which two persons may meet in this world of men: we can but exchange, from afar, despairing friendly signals, in the sure knowledge they will be misinterpreted. No soul may travel upon a bridge of words."

Thus spoke the Redeemer of Poictesme in an hour when he ought to have been specially happy; and yet knew that he was not happy; but merely very lonesome in the fond arms of a dear stranger.

Well, and I suspect that in this particular no one

of Manuel's race has ever greatly differed from their great progenitor. I believe it was then that Manuel spoke the final and all-comprehending words which every truth-loving male person may say to or about any woman. —Or, for that matter, about any other man.

A Note on Lichfield

IT WAS in sending forth a special edition of *The Cream of the Jest*, in which for the first time the art of Mr. Papé extenuated the inadequacies of the author, that I found it well to add to *The Cream of the Jest* an explanatory and yet not too dangerously explicit protest—about Lichfield.

The Lichfield of this comedy, and of yet other comedies, has been so often and so persistently located in Virginia that it probably is useless for me again to point out that in Virginia exists no post office of that name. There appears, indeed, to be nowhere in the United States of America any city or town, or even a village, called Lichfield.

The deduction should, thus, be fairly obvious, for every considerate person, that Lichfield, as well as Storisende, is to be found only in, as Richard Harrowby has phrased it, "that happy, harmless Fableland which is bounded by Avalon and Phæacia and Sea-Coast Bohemia, and the contiguous forests of Arden and Broceliande, and on the west by the Hesperides."

YET I, for one, have rather frequently speculated, during my writing of the five books relative to Lichfield, why the American descendants of Manuel and of Jurgen should all have elected to settle in such an out-of-the-way place. My concern hereabouts has been, to be sure, not wholly academic, not quite unselfish, inasmuch as the remoteness of Lichfield could not but make the compiling of these descendants' histories by any chronicler resident in Virginia additionally inconvenient. Had kindlier accident but removed the American descendants of Manuel to Norfolk or to Richmond, I have reflected—or even to Atlanta or Jacksonville or Little Rock—or, for that matter, to any city whatsoever within the States which geographers ordinarily catalogue as Southern,—then my contemporaries among the twenty-third generation of this family would have been more accessible. Their actions would have been far easier to observe. The costs of a visit to them would have been esteemed, by any fair-minded Commissioner of Internal Revenue, a legitimate expense in the conduct of my business. And moreover, instead of leading a comparatively starveling existence, in that mere backwater of a Lichfield, their lives would have been glorified by contact with one or another of the above-alluded-to cities' material and cultural splendors and unexampled progress since the War Between the States,—pre-eminencies in which our Lichfield has rather notably lacked.

"Why can you not live"—I have inquired very
often of the latter-day Manuelites—"in some town
which is more generally known? Why need your
names be encounterable in the telephone directory of
no place which a greater number of people have
visited, and in which they consequently take a quasi-
personal interest? My publishers assure me that the
effect upon sales would be highly gratifying. Now in
candor, and in example also, I admit the advantages
of living in a Southern climate. Yet why can you not
live in one or another Southern city a thought more
familiar to everybody, and to me too, so that I might
record your doings against an at once recognizable
background of local facts and civic traditions and
customs and foibles and general polity? Why have
you, in fine, compelled me always to write about this
Lichfield which, when my writing was done, nobody
could quite certainly identify as any special Southern
city?"

But they one and all evade an answer, replying only
that it is out of their forethought for me. These
Kennastons and Harrowbys and Hugonins—these
Musgraves and these Townsends—have not ever
given me any more rational and frank response to
that inquiry, as to why the American inheritors of
Manuel's blood all live in Lichfield?

Instead, the Manuelites evade me, with a wise
smiling, almost tacitly. When they speak, it is about
such seemingly irrelevant matters as the Louisianian

romances of George Washington Cable, which
brought about his exile from the South; or about a
Richard Bale of Balisand who lived in Gloucester
County, Virginia, with a modern frankness found
nauseous by the Virginian gentry; or about that
Hard-Boiled Virgin who traduced Atlanta and
Charleston by not representing both of these cities
as the supreme flowering of American culture. Privily
they talk, in the hushed voice of one whose speech
fares into purlieus wherein imagination dare not
dwell, about that H. L. Mencken who wrote, in The
Sahara of the Bozart, a most infamous libel which
suggested that the South did not excel every other
section of this country in art as well as in all other
praiseworthy activities. And they whisper also about
that Englishman, John Drinkwater, who first placed
upon the stage at Richmond-in-Virginia a drama
which provoked mass-meetings among the Daughters
of the Confederacy by representing General Robert
E. Lee as wearing a beard a full two months before
General Lee did wear a beard. The failure of our
country to declare war against Great Britain after
this unparalleled calumny is still regarded, in Richmond-in-Virginia, as one of the more murky episodes
of American history.

JOHN CHARTERIS, though—I now recall—did once
go a bit farther, and did refer me to the eleventh

fable in his own *Foolish Prince.* That apologue I
therefore append in this place, as the sole answer
which I have ever been able to extort from these
over-willful characters who will not permit me to
write about any real Southern city.

Now the fable is called

P r e h i s t o r i c s

As was the manner of those far-off days, the traveler came mounted upon a hippogriffin to the bronze
gates of a walled city. "And I have often heard of
your city," he said, when he had inspected the place;
"but not one-tenth of its wonders,"—he added, upon
the excellent principle that there is nothing like the
decimal system—"had ever been told to me."

They answered him, modestly, as was the manner
of those far-off days:

"Indeed, we cannot deny that our city was the
cradle of this nation, or that it was the first begetter
of all civil and religious liberty, of statesmanship
and patriotism and every virtue, or that it is the only
stronghold, in these degenerate times, of exalted culture and morality. We cannot deny our men are the
bravest and most chivalrous that have ever lived, our
women the most beautiful and chaste. Nay, more than
this! because of our exceedingly great love for truth-
fulness we cannot even deny that no other place
shows in the past a history so soul-inspiring as does
our city; that to-day no other place may be compared

with us in prosperity or in contentment or in our wholesome way of living; and that never at any time in the future shall any other city equal the least of our glories."

"Now I also, no word of this do I deny," replied the traveler, with such frank enthusiasm as was the manner of those far-off days. "For many excellences do I unfeignedly admire you and your city. Yet ———"

—Whereafter, very promptly, lest that "yet" should prove the beginning of a hint as to their city's displaying some fault, they abolished the traveler and his hippogriffin also, with large paving stones, as was the manner of those far-off days.

Townsend of Lichfield

VERY long ago did I select the punning title, *Townsend of Lichfield*, for that book which was to have continued *The Cords of Vanity*, and which would have brought the literary career of Robert Etheridge Townsend to its full flowering, and which would have concluded the Biography of the Life of Manuel as a narrative. Yet *Townsend of Lichfield* is a book you will not ever read. I lament that fact in all sincerity, because the book would have annoyed such a great host of people whom it is really one's altruistic duty to annoy . . . I had looked forward to a liberal dealing with real persons—presented under such pseudonyms as would ward off libel suits without ever becoming in the least impervious,—and to some salutary loosing of long-pent-up malice, in this intended handling of the contemporary life of Lichfield during the last twenty-five years, and in this handling, also, of certain chicaneries and small droll happenings in the literary world of America during the same period.

But I was entrapped into writing *The Jewel Mer-*

chants. Then *Domnei* and *The Cream of the Jest*
proved each too short to make a fair sized volume
in the Storisende edition. To accompany *Domnei* I
therefore wrote out, in 1926, *The Music from Behind the Moon,* and a trifle later, in 1929, completed
the trilogy of *The Witch-Woman* in time for its last
two sections to appear in the final volume of the
Storisende edition. And to *The Cream of the Jest*
was added, naturally enough, *The Lineage of Lichfield,* as an epitome which alike records and disposes
of all the inheritors of Dom Manuel's life with whom
the Biography has held traffic.

Yet the result was that in this way, without quite
expecting it, one found the Biography to contain
twenty units, with an additional volume of odds and
ends thrown in to serve, as it were, as an appendix
of explanatory notes. Beyond twenty units the Biography could not well extend, in the teeth of the fixed
law of Poictesme that all things must go by tens forever. Here discretion joined forces with mercy; since
both these abstractions forbid me to overtax the
gentleness of the gentle reader by requesting him to
read thirty volumes hand-running.

It followed, in immutable logic, that *Townsend of
Lichfield,* as well as seven stories about the witch-
woman, must remain in John Charteris' library,
among the unwritten books, along with I do not now
remember how many other volumes which I began as
a part of the Biography and did not ever finish.

PAUSING here, I look back in memory upon those various other books which, once, were to have been a part of the Biography of the Life of Manuel, and which for one reason or another reason did not ever get written . . . As to the burning of the first version of *Something About Eve*, and the abridgment of *The Witch-Woman* into a trilogy, I have already spoken in discussing these two volumes. Besides, both of these books did eventually get into type; and they so stand on a rather different plane.

But, as far back as 1905, the first *Romance of Lusignan* was destroyed. Some of the most scholarly looking notes made for this story yet survive the long-perished manuscript; and they abound in such impressive references to mediæval literature that it seems a large pity these notes cannot be used somehow. This romance, it should here be explained, had not anything to do with the book now known as *Domnei*; but instead dealt with the amours of Hugh de Lusignan and Isabella of Angoulême, who married, first, King John of England at a time when she was betrothed to Lusignan, and twenty years afterward married Lusignan, who was at the time betrothed to her daughter . . . For at this season I intended that Isabella of Angoulême, with the connivance of her two husbands, should become the ancestress of all the characters in the Biography, and should play in some sort the part more lately allotted to Dom Manuel. But this plan about Dame

Isabella proved a false start, howsoever engaging appeared her story in itself. I found that I must deal, all through the Biography, with a man's life from a male point of view; and, as Chloris has acutely remarked, an ancestress is always feminine.

In 1908 was destroyed a novel dealing with the Earl of Pevensey who flourished in England under King Charles the Second. About this story, which seems not ever to have had a finally chosen title, I can remember very little save that my protagonist pursued, among other ladies, the not obdurate Duchesse de la Rivière, whose daughter Carola, some years later, in *The High Place*, became the first wife of Florian de Puysange. Although some fragments of this story survive, in Olivia's Pottage, no notes made for the novel exist; and I believe that not much of it was ever written.

But a well-nigh completed novel was burned in 1913. This book concerned the married life of Cynthia Allonby and Edward Musgrave (both of whom are to be encountered in Porcelain Cups, apart from the possibility that this Cynthia may figure also in Judith's Creed) and it told of their emigration to America. But the tale itself dealt rather with their second daughter, Katherine Musgrave, who was wooed by such august persons as George Villiers, Duke of Buckingham, and by Henry Stuart, Prince of Wales (who did not truly die in 1612, if this chronicle was to be believed, but survived incognito,

under the name of Gervase Woods), and by Opech-
ancanough, the Indian Emperor of Paumunkey.

This story seems to me, in retrospection, to have
had fair possibilities. It began in St. Helen's church-
yard, at Abingdon in Berkshire, and it ended at
Natural Bridge in Virginia. And that was the precise trouble with it: the story dealt with real places
at an actual time. So this romance was sacrificed in
the end, just as the story about Pevensey had been
sacrificed—in the end—to my resolve, as formed
during the completing of *Gallantry*, to avoid, in so
far as was humanly possible, ever laying the scene
of any story in a milieu which I myself had not created. I needed in my own little world to be omnipo-
tent, and to move untrammeled by historic facts which
any demiurge other than I had brought into being.
So, after desperately endowing America with another English settlement contemporaneous with
Jamestown, and after finding that this device simply
would not do, I destroyed all: and I went back to
work upon *The Strength of the Hills*.

But this too, in 1914, was destroyed . . . *The
Strength of the Hills* was a modern romance which
dealt mainly with Cynthia Musgrave and with that
George Bulmer who appears, not very importantly,
in *The Cords of Vanity*, as Mr. Townsend's uncle.
In the background of the comedy was a most re-
grettable story of embezzlement and incest; Dame
Venus herself, that lady of the hollow hill (who was

now resident among hills less completely hollow, in that they were merely tunneled for coal mining) figured in this story; and it all ended in Cynthia's marrying, not George Bulmer, but one of the Chaytors: this much alone I can remember about *The Strength of the Hills*.

Then also I once wrote out a good part of the story of Wilhelmina Musgrave. I did not finish it. I intended, after all, to go on living in Virginia, in which commonwealth the facts of the story I had in mind are so widely known that any relating of these facts in print would beget fury among her rather numerous descendants and a host of high-minded editorials in the newspapers of Virginia as to this foul slandering of the South's aristocracy . . . Moreover do I recall the partially written book about Lord Hervey—I refer to Pope's "Sporus,"—and that other never finished book about Katherine Parr and her four husbands; and that story of Ninzian's part in the colonization of America, whereby he earned his pardon from Lucifer; and the ten tales concerned with Richard Harrowby's adventurings in the occult; and the modern dizain about Lichfield . . . Yes, off and on, I have contributed a sizeable number of volumes to the library of John Charteris,—of which books (inasmuch as he too is an author) he must read most frequently, I am certain, that book which was to have been about John Charteris.

Yet I daresay that Charteris himself, as well as

every other author, has contributed to that blessed library at least a volume or two: and we each know how excellent are all those books which we planned and did not ever write.

LET us therefore give hearty thanks for those books which we planned and did not ever write. Such was their happy fate that against their loveliness no compositor has upraised his impious blunt pencil, to question either their grammar or their spelling, or to demand Procrustean operations upon their perfected prose. These books did not come back to us in proof sheets bescribbled with insane suggestions in blue and eruptive with the uncivil verdant comment, "This page is one line too long." Not ever were their chapter endings marred with the brisk and over-businesslike order in green ink, "Add something here to make five lines."

Nowhere in these books did any printer's error cunningly elude our eyes through all the long, laborious proof-reading until at last, from the fair page of an irrevocably manufactured volume, that error, in triumphant enormity, might skip forth like a very tiny coal-black fiend. These books were not printed upon paper which scattered in the reader's lap white dust. No least fault bedimmed the beauty of those books which we planned and, for one reason or another reason, did not ever write.

Nor did any criticaster mishandle them. They alone of our books, were not put in their proper and unenviable place by the indubious godlings who are quite certain about all things which be, saving only the truism that if their judgments had value they themselves would not be writing what they describe as "critiques" for the local Sunday paper. Nor did these books evoke fine pæans which so belauded our excellence, in such wholly handsome superlatives, that we for a glad while had read on beamingly, well into the third paragraph, before being smitten down by the knowledge that only a well-meaning rustic idiot could have written those last five lines.

These books escaped all ills. They were not praised by them who still take Karl Marx rather seriously; nor did William Lyon Phelps at any time asperse their literary merits with his approval. The Book of the Month Club respectfully ignored them as it pimped for the inane among the illiterate. They were not awarded a Pulitzer Prize. They were honored in all ways, were those books which we planned and, for one reason or another reason, did not ever write.

So is it that to-day not even their contrivers can discover in these books any flaw. These books do not raise the untactful questions: "What butterfingers could have let this adverb thus slip its moorings and settle here, of all places, where it adheres to the wrong word? What bungler thus divorced this pronoun from its noun? However came this sentence to

end with a phrase of so grave unimportance? What
kleptomaniac pilfered hence a comma? And how, in
Jehovah's most high name, did anybody ever come
to write so very maladroitly any such moonstruck
nonsense as maunders through those wholly dreadful last five lines?"

They only of our books do not humiliate us. They
repay not any months and no years of labor by ar-
raigning us, in every printed page, upon the double
counts of time-wasting and of botchery. They stay
forever beautiful, and urbane, and they are always
kindlily companionable, those books which we
planned and, for one reason or another reason, did
not ever write.

WELL, but *Townsend of Lichfield*, to go back a bit,
was to have dealt with Mr. Townsend's personal observations as to American letters since 1903 and as
to life in Lichfield during the same period; and it was
to handle both themes candidly. So I daresay that,
for my own comfort's sake, it is quite as well that
the book failed to get written.

It would not, of course, have been an especially
notable book,—if but because in creative writing, as
I have previously pointed out, no instance of first-
class art has ever been a truthful reproduction of the
artist's own era . . . In passing, this is a statement
which so many have derided as to make the circum-

stance seem mildly curious that no one of these
deriders has educed any such instances of first-class
art, in any of fiction's various branches, as would
seem to deny this fact . . . Yet *Townsend of Lichfield*, howsoever remote from a masterpiece, would
have been a peculiarly diverting book to write. It
would have gratified my curiosity, for one matter,
in that it would have enabled me to find out whether
or no Mr. Townsend ever married Bettie Hamlyn.
And it would have summed up, as fairly as I could,
the comedy of my own generation in American letters and the comedy of my own generation in the
life of Lichfield.

It would thus have dealt with a state of affairs,
and with an entire civilization, now utterly done
with: for its punning title would have been well justified, now that the Lichfield about which I have
written so much is as thoroughly bygone as is Poictesme. Moreover, the book would have had for the
younger generation a very positive historic value. It
would thus have been, perhaps to a greater degree
than *The Way of Ecben*, an appropriate thesis to
commemorate my leave-taking of the younger generation alike in art and in letters.

So do I approach unavoidably a theme which nobody can approach with any real profit. I mean, the
younger generation. I mean that the conduct of the
younger generation is a topic concerning which the
sole possible verdict to be rendered from the more

sedate side of forty was long ago fixed by adamantean usage, from which one does not dare deviate.

For to time-ripened judgment the activities of the younger generation have always been, without any exception, a sign of world-wide degeneracy. To the more elderly of all eras has this dreadful fact been apparent ever since these frivolously modern activities provoked the Deluge; as yet afterward the behavior of the younger generation brought about the decadence of Rome—*ætas parentum tulit nos nequiores,* you may find Horace lamenting at about the time, quaintly enough, of Christ's birth; and enraged Dante; and upset John Milton into reams of marmoreal blank verse; and at a still later period aggrieved the Old Woman Who Lived in a Shoe.

From the beginning, it would seem, all really matured opinion has been at one on the point that the younger generation was speeding post-haste to the dogs. Since the commencement of recorded literature, in any event, full proof has not been lacking that oldsters everywhere, in every known era, have drawn a snarling comfort from this pronouncement, just as pertinaciously, and just as pathetically, as the world's current youth has always been positive that, when once everybody over fifty was disposed of, the human race was bound for the millennium around the next corner but one.

It is true that, in practice, the younger generation appears to reach middle-age before it quite reaches

either the dogs or the millennium; and then of
course it replaces the fallacies of youth with such
substitutes for logic as middle-age finds acceptable
whensoever it discourses as to yet another pesti-
ferous younger generation . . . But of middle-age
I intend to speak later. Meanwhile, so far as I may
conjecture, the younger generation has always passed
through its so brief career in a never-failing excitement,—an excitement roused by the discovery that
the existence of God is open to dispute, but that the
pleasures of coition are not.

I can well recall that in my own Victorian first
heyday these facts were known. They were not, to
be sure, very often encountered in print: but in the
conversation of the young, and especially in, as it
were, co-educational tête-à-têtes, I am afraid that no
themes were more familiar.

THAT fictitious city which I have called Lichfield may
have differed, of course, from all other places; yet
I think it did not; and I really cannot remember that
in our late-Victorian, entirely imaginary Lichfield
(McKinley being Consul) young persons when left
to themselves were over-rigorously hampered either
in speech or action. Certain words one avoided: but
all these had many synonyms, apart from the fact
that the things they stood for could be made, and
were made, livelily communicative in pantomime. In

brief, all our unlegalized and callow, but our con-
summated, amours were conducted with a civil fur-
tiveness, which yet, in the last outcome, did not demand of anybody concerned any special amount of
concealment.

One found instead that society at large was here,
in a benevolent and slightly flustered way, intent to
ignore what was plain enough. One's elders, for their
own reasons, preferred to remain conveniently blind.
Approaching now in reverie the era of the greater
Roosevelt, one found that intelligent husbands and
intelligent parents had every logical reason to avoid
making any such discoveries as they, in either capacity, would be called on to avenge at the cost of an
open scandal. It followed that the well-bred husband
or the properly reared parent—in Lichfield—whensoever visited by unavoidable suspicions, was at polite pains not to verify them.

For, in this concededly fictitious city, we had the
rule of thumb, to which I have elsewhere alluded in
the stories about Lichfield, that "immoral" conduct
did not exist until after some public mention of it had
been printed in one of the local newspapers . . . It
is an odd fact that to be mentioned in a New York
paper, as the mishaps of Lichfield now and then were
mentioned (with those Northerners' notorious lack
of good breeding), did not count. One could ignore
that; one could pretend not to have seen it: and one
did . . . Meanwhile, fairly well-connected persons

could have pretty much anything "kept out of the papers"—out of, that is, the only two papers which counted—short of a murder or a suicide. Neither, I rejoice to report, occurred over-frequently in the best circles. And besides, whensoever among really nice people alcohol or the divided affections of a gentle-woman did result in an undeniable murder, then the police were conveniently obtuse about finding any clues as to its perpetrator, and the whole affair was dropped quickly: whereas a suicide, when committed by a person of sufficiently high social standing, was described always in print, with the abettance of our tactful coroner, as a regrettable accident.

Embezzlements also, now that I think of it, were awkward, because they necessitated a brief paragraph in both local papers: yet this was printed inconspicu-ously, on the second or third page of the paper, where, again, you could loyally pretend not to have seen it. I can recall a veritable epidemic of embezzle-ments committed by junior members of the leading Lichfieldian families. But I recall too that every difficulty of this nature was quietly settled out of court, and that nobody went to jail for it. The jail was for colored people . . . As concerns adultery and fornication among mature persons who moved in really good social circles, I cannot describe Lich-field's attitude toward such matters any more clearly than I have already done in *The Rivet in Grand-father's Neck* and in *Something About Eve*. Such

improprieties, howsoever widely known, or howsoever freely discussed in private conversation, were
nevertheless assumed, as a social rule of thumb,
simply not to exist among the well-bred; and they
were thus comfortably disposed of, through this
bland assumption, without ever troubling anybody's
home life or moral standards. The oligarchy of Lichfield, in fine, was held together with innumerable
small bonds of mutual silence.

Under such a régime—the collapse of which *Townsend of Lichfield* was to have depicted—the younger
generation was more quiet than are its present-day
successors in Lichfield and in all other places. Yet I
cannot assert that, beneath this relative quietness, it
was any the less sophisticated, in its own somewhat
hole-and-corner way; or that in the back parlors of
Lichfield, after the gas jets had been turned down
into very tiny cones of blue flame, which spluttered
as if in remonstrance every once in a while, the
younger generation then displayed upon sofas, which
were a bit too narrow for complete comfort, any
morbid amount of self-repression.

I INCLINE, in short, to think that in human economy
the younger generation has always remained a tolerably staple product. Its language varies, as does also
perhaps, at times, the pitch of its voice: but its
theme does not vary. Its age-old theme is, always, a

restatement of the truism that its elders have lied about most matters, and have mismanaged all matters, beyond human endurance. And its mistake is—always—to believe that the lying and the mismanagement may by-and-by be remedied.

For youth, to the one side, has faith and hope. But middle-age tends rather to dismiss these two cardinal virtues in favor of charity. Youth, in a less happy aspect, is heir to the superior pleasures of pessimism and to the warm gustos of moral indignation; but middle-age has mastered that invaluable gesture which is known as a shrug.

Meanwhile, until forty-five or thereabouts, no man has any first-hand knowledge as to the average of human life, through the sufficing reason that he has seen but tatters and small scattered segments of the affair. At forty-five, though, he has watched his own thinned generation straggle into maturity, and the generation of his parents filed away in caskets. Old age still remains to be endured—perhaps. But he has observed it, day by day, through near half a century; he has seen his elders pass, by the hundreds, baffled and withered and yet, in some pathetic way, content enough: so that he knows in general terms what old age too is like.

Thus does it come about that to whosoever reaches forty-five the entire average course of human life has been displayed in somewhat the bewildering fashion of a moving picture of which the first and the second halves are being shown simultaneously on the same screen. The spectator has got little enough out of it, God knows. Even so, he has his own sad advantage in knowledge over those persons who have not yet witnessed the inconsequent, astounding jumble. He at least has perceived it all with his own senses: he has perceived, with an immediacy which no report can parallel, what actually does befall the average man between the hours of birth and death: and it remains an affair of which his knowledge, howsoever blurred and howsoever limited, comes to him at first hand. He is not dependent, as his juniors yet stay necessarily dependent, as even the superior thirties yet stay dependent, upon guess-work and the statements of other persons . . . Or let us vary the figure. Let us say that a traveller who has made a journey, it matters not how unperceptive his nature, does, after all, know more about that particular journey than is ever revealed to the most faithful and the most imaginative student of guidebooks.

Thus, I repeat, the average of human life has been shown in its entirety to every man of forty-five. The verdicts then vary: but you may note, even so, the cynic and the pessimist to turn unaccountably mellow. Life, it would seem, like a trip to the dentist, is not so very bad, after all, once you have put up with it. Life does not bid fair, to the tiring eyes of forty-five, ever to become a perfect business; and to preserve any special altruism at forty-five is to present a happily rare case of arrested development. But the point is that when the performance has been witnessed in its entirety, with one's own senses, then the average of human life does tend to seem well enough just as it stands. The lying and the mismanagement do not promise ever to be rectified: but that appears hardly an elegiac matter, after all; for middle-age, I repeat, has mastered that invaluable gesture which is known as a shrug.

Such is the discovery made by all men at forty-five or thereabouts: such, if you so prefer to phrase it, is the illusion to which middle-age becomes a victim: such, in any case, is the eternal crux between middle-age and youth. Youth is credulous; and youth is amenable to persuasion in a disastrously large number of matters. Yet upon one single issue youth stays as iron and granite: youth does not ever believe that life serves well enough just as it stands. To conjecture that such is just possibly the case remains the attested hall-mark of middle life . . . Thereafter optimism develops insidiously; and the more lucky among us sink, cackling thinly, into an amiable senescence.

BUT it is with the younger generation in letters, rather than in life, that I am here the more distinctly concerned, now that time has dissevered me from both. This never written *Townsend of Lichfield* was to have made plain the fact of there being in literary fields an offset to that particular bit of knowledge just now referred to as being acquired by most men at forty-five. It is that any writer who thus comes to forty-five has purchased his knowledge without—at best—improving upon his chances to communicate this knowledge.

For, after forty-five or thereabouts, it is inevitable that a writer should cease to develop as a writer, just as he ceases to develop as a mammal. No one of his faculties, whatsoever else may happen to them, can improve after that all-arresting date. Some few—although not many authors, it more or less inexplicably appears—begin to fail earlier. But the average writer has reached his peak at, to my finding, forty; and with favoring luck, with all that he has learned of technique to counterbalance a perhaps lessened exuberance in creative power, he may retain that peak for some years. Yet this retention profits him little. He has nothing new to give: and you may look henceforward to get from him no surprises.

Ultimately this does not matter: and, where the writer is at all remembered, posterity selects, in a rough-and-ready and a very often wrong-headed fashion, that which posterity esteems to be the best of this writer's work, without any need to bother over the relative order of the work's composition, or to think about the writer's age at the time when he allowed himself the diversion of doing this or the other particular bit of writing. But during the remainder of the man's career as a practising author, and during the remainder of his stay upon earth, this individuality which permeates the work of every writer worth his salt, and which keeps the exercises of an authentic genius always homogeneous, does matter a great deal, to the debit side of the ledger.

For we ask—not at all illogically—that a new book shall contain something new. We expect, in fine, some element of surprise: and after a writer's style is fairly formed, after his talents have each been competently developed, that is precisely the one element which he cannot supply. There is, from his point of view, no reason why he should supply it. He is still—so does he think, perhaps rightly, perhaps in merciful illusion—still at his best, such as that best is. Yet, even be he right, each book that he publishes is a disappointment, howsoever loyally concealed, to his readers; and his most excellent work can no longer produce upon his readers the same effect, the old startling wonderment, simply because his special excellence is familiar.

Every considerate person must respect, for example, the genius of Rudyard Kipling and of Bernard Shaw, and upon a lower plane the genius of H. G. Wells and of Arnold Bennett: yet for how many years has the publication of a new book by

any of them been an event in which it was not possible to take real interest. For how many years have
we at bottom deplored the exercise of their genius.
And so it is with every writer whose manner has
been admirable long enough to become familiar. He
publishes perforce a book which in every essential
we have already read, time and again. We purchase
(or it may be that we do but tender a more thrifty
homage in the form of asking for his last new opus
at the free public library) in fealty to old delight.
But we labor through our reading of the sunken
deity's self-repetitions with a sort of unadmitted
impatience, and with an unacknowledged surfeit, by
which those braver persons who write book reviews
are irritated a great deal more openly.

Meanwhile the report gets about that the man
is making money out of his writing: and in the cor-
rupting miasma of that rumor no literary repu-
tation, howsoever lusty, can long survive. So does it
follow that by the time a tolerably successful artist
in letters is really in full control of his powers, such
as they are, he is definitely, for the rest of his lifetime, outmoded. In fact, he has become in some sort
a pest.

There is loss here for the reader, though, I confess, I can see no possible way out. But for the
artist there is no weighty loss, and no valid ground
upon which, as it were, to repine. Every artist in
letters must become, ere he reaches sixty, more or

less of a nuisance to the world of current reading-matter: but that, after all, is not an affair with which he himself is concerned vitally. This sybarite spoils paper, as I have elsewhere tried to explain, for his own diversion: he knows that the artist, lucky above all men and alone among mortal beings, is sometimes, if only for a season, praised, and even is paid sound money, for diverting himself: and he knows too that to the artist, when the applause lessens and the autograph hunters depart to ring other door-bells, there remains still the chance—granted to him alone of all mortal beings—to continue to divert himself in precisely that way which he most prefers.

But from the front ranks of contemporary writers, from the ranks of those who exercise an actually vivid and yet-growing influence, an author at about the time of his fiftieth birthday must withdraw perforce. It matters not (for the while) whether his writing now be better or be worse than it was in that forever occluded time when the manner of his writing appeared new. That manner has become, to his contemporaries, hackneyed. And so the real interest of his contemporaries has been turned—again, perforce—to those younger writers who have at least the one indispensable quality. They are new.

MEANWHILE I have said, "The average writer has reached his peak at, to my finding, forty: and with

favoring luck, with all that he has learned of technique to counterbalance a perhaps lessened exuberance in creative power, he may retain that peak for
some years." The trouble is that he does not retain
it indefinitely: the trouble is that in no great while
the creative power is quite surely lessened; and the
technique does but play futilely with the picked
bones of defunct talents. The trouble is, in brief,
that even for the most prodigally gifted of creative
writers the way lies, by-and-by, downhill forever.

It has been the fate of but too many of our more
captivating prosateurs to outlive their powers
(which was a venial and perhaps an unavoidable
happening), and to outlive the desire to write, and
yet, whether out of sheer habit or out of man's
normal need for an income, to go on writing,—
which was in all respects a calamity. Here my theme
becomes difficult. To name here the living were uncivil. It is politely possible, though, to point in one
embracing gesture toward the supreme trinity of
English novel-writers, toward Scott and Dickens
and Thackeray—inasmuch as their merits nowadays have no least concern with the demerits of
Count Robert of Paris or of *Edwin Drood* or of
Philip,—and it is permissible to recall the arid in-
feriority of these dead giants' later labors without
any more of human pleasure than we unavoidably get
from our betters' downfall.

It is possible, too, to let the last-named writer

speak for the three of them. "All I can do now," said Thackeray—at about the time of his fiftieth birthday—"is to bring out my old puppets, and put new bits of ribbon on them. I have told my tale in the novel department. I only repeat old things in a pleasant way. I have nothing new to say. I get sick of my task when I am ill, and I think, 'Good Heavens! what is all this story about?' "

It is a query which has been echoed by his readers, and by the readers of Dickens, and by the readers of Scott, and by the readers of many another ageing novelist . . . I pause here. I am tempted. But I reflect, rather wistfully, that I had resolved to name in this place no living American author.

I somewhat regret that resolve. I would much like here to speak frankly of my own generation in American letters. For it was, in so far as it stays at all memorable, the first generation which criticized the polity of the United States. It was the first generation which said flatly, All is not well with this civilization. And it was, pre-eminently, the generation which destroyed taboos,—not all taboos, of course, but a great many of those fetishes which the preceding generations had all left in unmolested honor.

To the other side, it is a generation of which the present-day survivors appear, to my finding, a bit ludicrously to go on fighting battles that were won long ago. That civilization which they criticized

with harsh venom is extinct; and the all-terrifying
taboos against which they rode forth to battle have
been transmogrified into matters of sedate interest
to the antiquary. Yet does my generation evince a
tendency to preserve the posture of Ajax defying
the lightnings, under an unclouded sky. It has thus
become a depressingly comic spectacle. It has done
its work successfully: and that gratifying fact is the
one fact which this generation of writers who prided
themselves upon facing all facts, will not face to-
day. Instead, it goes on working at its some-while-
since finished job; and it tilts at dead dragons,
rather dodderingly, in the beginning palsy of super-
annuation.

So is it that, speaking always under the correction
of time, I would say this is a generation destined
quite quickly to be huddled away into oblivion by
man's common-sense. For this generation has said,
All is not well. To say that is permitted: to say that
is indeed a conventional gambit in every known
branch of writing. But this generation thereafter
proffered no panacea: and that special form of reticence is not long permissible. To the contrary it is
plain here that, just as Manuel told Coth, the dream
is better. It is man's nature to seek the dream; he
requires an ever-present recipe for the millennium;
and he vitally needs faith in some panacea or another
which by-and-by will correct all ills. This generation
has proffered no such recipe: and that queer omis-

sion has suggested, howsoever obliquely, that just
possibly no panacea may exist anywhere.

This is a truth which man's intelligence can confront for no long while. He very much prefers that
equivalent of hashish which I have seen described,
in the better-thought-of and more tedious periodi-
cals, as constructive criticism. Most properly, therefore, have those junior writers who were not ever
harried by taboos, or by the draft laws, begun to
suggest a tasteful variety of panaceas: and all persons blessed with common-sense will eventually select, if but at random, some one or another of these
recipes, wherein to invest faith and wherefrom to
extract comfort.

Meanwhile must all these intelligent seekers after
mental contentment put out of mind, as quickly as
may be possible, that unique and bothersome generation of writers who suggested no panacea . . . And
meanwhile also, as I remarked above, I intend here
to say not anything about this generation, which
Townsend of Lichfield would have commemorated
with candor,—if but because in a small book called
Some of Us I have said my say as to this same
generation with a great deal of tact.

But I divagate. These merely personal considerations have led me some little way from my main
point as to ageing writers. My point is simply this:
in rough figures all the available evidence goes to
show that after fifty the professional creative

writer is but too apt to labor in an ever-thickening shadow of decadence. There may be exceptions to this rule, as there are exceptions to every other rule; yet I believe that, if they indeed exist, they are few: and in any case one does not build upon exceptions.

IN 1920, therefore—by which time I was at work on my thirteenth volume, in *Figures of Earth*—I determined to finish the Biography of the Life of Manuel before I had passed fifty, if my own life should happen to last that long; and afterward to add no line to, and to change in nothing, the Biography. I labored then to that purpose, for some nine more years; it was a sort of three-handed game at which I gambled with Time and Chance, and won modestly, inasmuch as at the appointed date the Biography seemed, to my partial gaze, a completed and individual book as it now exists in the Storisende edition of the Biography.

Townsend of Lichfield I had not written, nor was *The Witch-Woman* shaped exactly as I had first planned it. That was the price paid for revising every volume of the Biography, yet once more, when I got together this Storisende edition. Nevertheless had I managed to achieve a symmetrical and organic whole in this somewhat appallingly large book, I reflected, as I fitted in the very last bit of the Biography, in the shape of *The Way of Ecben*.

Yes, the Biography, whatsoever its many demerits, displayed at any rate the virtue of unity. It displayed also the virtue of being finished and quite done with; so that I was now entitled to add, in all due reverence, as the final word to the long life of the Redeemer of Poictesme, *"Tetélestai!"*

With that which futurely I might or might not publish, the Biography of the Life of Manuel would be in no way connected: and neither with the Biography's merits nor with its faults had I any further concern. I merely knew it was the best and most carefully perfected writing which could be achieved by the limited talents, within the just as rigorously limited time, allotted to me as a human being. I knew that to complete the Biography had been what I most wanted to do. I knew that I had done it.

It followed that, although I honestly regretted I could not ever write *Townsend of Lichfield*—that philanthropic fine book which, as I remarked at outset, would have annoyed such a great host of people whom it is really one's altruistic duty to annoy,— yet, now that my plaything faced me in its completeness, like a finished cross-word puzzle to which in the proper place I had just added the last word, I was well content with the Biography. I would have you observe, though, that I was content upon entirely unliterary grounds. I was content because this toy had been to me a source of never-failing diversion for some twenty-eight years; therefore was I content; therefore was my individual and my only sentiment toward the Biography a glow of warm gratitude. The sentiments of all other persons as to this insufferably long book were, by the very worst of luck, beyond my control, now that I took leave of the Biography, and of my twenty-eight years' playing with it.

EXPLICIT

www.ingramcontent.com/pod-product-compliance
Lightning Source LLC
Chambersburg PA
CBHW031236090426
42742CB00007B/221